A GENEROUS LIFE

A GENEROUS *Life*

(*applause not included*)

BY KEVIN STIRRATT

BEACON HILL PRESS
O F   K A N S A S   C I T Y

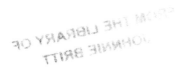
Copyright 2012
by Kevin Stirratt and Beacon Hill Press of Kansas City

ISBN 978-0-8341-2798-2

Printed in the
United States of America

Cover Design: Arthur Cherry
Interior Design: Sharon Page

Library of Congress Cataloging-in-Publication Data
Stirratt, Kevin, 1967-
    A generous life : applause not included / Kevin Stirratt.
      pages cm
    Includes bibliographical reference.
    ISBN 978-0-8341-2798-2 (pbk.)
    1. Generosity—Religious aspects—Christianity. 2. Christian life. I. Title.
    BV4647.G45S85 2012
    241'.4—dc23
                                                                    2011048836

10 9 8 7 6 5 4 3 2 1

CONTENTS

ACKNOWLEDGMENTS

I want to thank the many people who have had a hand in bringing this book from dream to reality. Greg Clark, Joyce Poeppelmeyer, Darrell Poeppelmeyer, Ralph Scherer, Kevin Sneed, Michaelle Stirratt, Mellissa Wass, and Lori Willis have all provided challenging questions, insights, and wonderful stories that have made this work more than I dreamed possible.

To my wife, Diana, and my boys, Andrew and Daniel: your patience during the long hours of writing was more than sacrificial. You generously gave of yourself by allowing me the time to fulfill God's call on my life in this work.

To the staff at Segue Foundation and Indiana Wesleyan University: I offer my sincerest thanks for your patience. You believed in this part of my ministry enough to allow me the time necessary to invest in this effort.

To Bonnie Perry and the Beacon Hill Press publishing team: I once again am humbled by your belief and encouragement. You are a gift God has used to confirm His call on my heart.

FOREWORD

It is a familiar scene. A mother and children fuss through the grocery. The kids are entertaining themselves as best they can, but it doesn't take long before the kids are bored and the mother is frustrated. That's when the negotiation begins. "If you will behave, I'll let you have a candy bar when we reach the checkout." That lasts a few aisles until their boredom escalates to misbehavior. That's when Mom gives up paying off the kids and moves to threats. "I'm going to tell your father how you are behaving. You kids are in so much trouble!"

Most of us grew up thinking this way—learning that we should be paid for good behavior and punished for bad behavior. We are trained to be "back-scratchers." *If I do something good for you, you should repay my generosity with some other act of kindness.*

Kevin Stirratt challenges us to reevaluate our understanding of generosity in our relationships and to embrace Jesus' call to keep giving when people don't deserve it.

In my forty years of work in pastoral ministry, I have written many books and taught thousands of people about the need to be generous with their possessions. It isn't often you find a book that challenges your thinking and expands your passion to give of yourself the way *A Generous Life* does.

I've known the author for many years and have had the blessing of encouraging and mentoring him on various occasions. His love for God and family are very evident in this book. Kevin has the unique ability to remind you of things you thought you already knew but say them in ways that strike a new chord of commitment in your heart. Kevin will push your understanding of Jesus' teachings and cause you to reevaluate how you express the love of Christ at home, at church, and in the world.

If you've been treated unfairly, wondered how to keep serving your family when you are getting nothing in return, struggled to cope with your children's selfish behavior, or felt alone in your willingness to keep giving of yourself at church or work, you need to read this book. You will burst out in laughter one second and cry in repentance the next.

Get ready for a life-changing spiritual journey into a life that reflects the generous love of Jesus!

Stan Toler

1
GENEROSITY OR BACK-SCRATCHING?

∽

That's Not Fair

"That's not fair!" It seems like it was the first full sentence my kids learned. How is it that a two year old who has barely learned to talk is so aware of the injustice in the world? Yet, we have all experienced the same indignation that children feel when they have been treated in a way they consider unjust.

It is true for all of us. We were born with the ability to fight against what we understand to be unjust. Nobody teaches toddlers to become angry when a sibling picks up their toy. They just know they want it and it isn't fair that they don't have it. Nobody has to teach the child that most trades aren't fair unless they have out-bartered their friend.

I watched my own children fight for what is fair. Andrew had the Hot Wheels® toy Daniel wanted.

"That's mine!"

"Offer him a trade, Daniel" was his mother's wise advice. He opened his hand and offered his brother a broken car he was ready to discard.

"No!" His brother was quite offended. "I want your best car."

Daniel's eyes scrunched with two-year-old temper. The fight was on.

I had hoped my children would outgrow this childishness. I've come to realize it has nothing to do with being a child and everything to do with being part of Adam's race. While they don't fight over toy cars anymore, my teenagers still race each other to the car.

"I call shotgun!"

"No, I got here first. You get in the back!"

"Too bad! I called it!"

I pray, *God why aren't they generous with each other? Why don't they put each other's feelings ahead of their own? Why do they refuse to give, but always take?*

I wish I were different, but I see the same tendency in my own heart. When I get home and am tired from the day the last thing I want to do is cook dinner or clean dishes. Someone else should do that. I'm exhausted. It's just not fair. At the end of a long week, I have the right to a restful Saturday! Right? After all, I worked hard, and I have needs too. It's my turn to be served. That's what is fair.

We're Born Back-scratchers

From birth, there is something in us that measures the world through this sense of fairness. My brother, Randy, and I were in elementary school. Our house had an old television antenna tower that was a perfect trellis for climbing up to the roof. Dad had told us many times to not do it, but he wasn't here and the snow was deep enough to make the jump thrilling! Randy had a snowsuit, but I only had a pair of jeans. The third and fourth jumps from the roof to the snowdrifts were just as much fun as the first and second. My jeans were soaked and my legs were beginning to sting, though not enough to quit the repeated climbs and jumps.

"Randy and Kevin! Get off that roof this instant!" Mom's voice shrilled with the threat of punishment. We considered it one more call to jump, and down we went. We thought it was far more comical than Mom did. She dragged us into the house and proceeded to inflict justice. I was first.

If you've ever experienced a spanking when your jeans are soaked with snow and ice, you understand that each swat stung more viciously than the last. I'm not sure how many I got, but I had one thrilling thought that made the pain bearable. My brother was going to get his, and I was going to get to watch!

Mom was still angry and Randy's eyes were wide with fear. She laid him on the bed face down, still garbed in his new snowsuit. The first whack sounded like a pillow strike in a pillow fight. *Woof.* It didn't sound very painful. I wondered what Randy was feeling. She tried again. His five-inch layer of stuffing was protecting him.

"I can't feel that!" Randy was now laughing.

Woof. She tried again, holding back a chuckle. Randy was almost singing with joy. "I can't feel that! I can't feel that!"

My mother has never lacked for a sense of humor, and this was more than she could take. The next few swats got progressively weaker as her cackles grew progressively louder. Within a few seconds she and Randy were both lying on the bed laughing. Her fury was gone, and Randy knew he had escaped his punishment.

My face burned with anger. This wasn't fair. I got mine and he needed to get his! We both were jumping and he needed to feel the same level of pain I had. "Spank him, Mom! Spank him!" I shouted at the top of my lungs. It only fueled my mother's laughter. Randy squealed, "I can't feel it!"

Mom roared.

It's a sore subject to this day. It wasn't fair. It didn't matter that I got what I deserved. That wasn't the point at all. I didn't get equal treatment. That was the point. I was treated unfairly because someone else received more mercy than I had. It wasn't fair because I had received more punishment than someone who deserved it just as much as I had. I didn't have to be schooled in injustice. I was living it.

While these injustices seem trivial, we all have experienced moments when the injustice is difficult. An exhausted husband who gets up grumpy disregards his wife's needs. A coworker manipulates a superior to get a promotion we are convinced is ours. Children disregard our sacrifices and accuse us of not caring enough to let them do what they want to do. Someone at church criticizes the ministry we have worked tirelessly to improve. A husband is unfaithful to his wife. A child steals from a parent. A mother abandons her family.

The abuses can be severe—so severe that Jesus' words strike us as completely unfair. "Turn the other cheek," "Go the extra mile," "Give your tunic as well," "Pray for those who persecute you," "Love your enemy."

Jesus is obviously approaching life from a different point of view. It is His perspective that will challenge us to keep giving when others would demand repayment.

A Different Perspective: Generosity vs. Reciprocity

Jesus challenges our sense of injustice with a call to generosity—to give back more than we have received. Give more than we are expected to give. Offer forgiveness and reconciliation in a measure that reflects the love the Father has lavished on us. Use a generous portion when we deliver grace, mercy, patience, and so on.

Jesus calls us to quit evaluating every relationship based on fair treatment and reminds us that He lavished His love on us when we didn't deserve it. His ultimate generosity calls us to walk away from our demand for equal treatment. He calls us to give when others want to take. He calls us to share when others want to hoard resources. He calls us to lavish love when others want to give only what is deserved. It goes against the very fabric of our natural selfish condition.

From the time we are born, we limit our generosity toward others. It doesn't take too much life experience before we begin honing our skills at keeping life as fair as possible. We know a good trade and a bad trade. We know when others are treating us unfairly. We are keenly aware of how we should be treated and horribly unaware of the injustice we inflict on others. We know when it is okay to give up on someone and walk away from the relationship. It all starts with childish competition, but in the end leaves us unable to experience the power of relationships in which everyone's needs are met. We are intended for blessing, but we live convinced we are supposed to get more than we have. We are back-scratchers, always limiting our love by what we expect to get in return. We live in a world based on reciprocity, not generosity.

Reciprocity is a big word that refers to equal treatment. You took my toy, so I took yours. That is reciprocity. You rubbed my back for two minutes, so I'm counting down the seconds while I rub yours. You got to watch your television show; now it's my turn to control the remote. I had to watch the kids all day yesterday, now you must let me have some alone time! You scratch my back, *then* I'll scratch yours. That is fair. That is reciprocity.

This "back-scratchers mentality" is how the world evaluates right and wrong. "An eye for an eye. A tooth for a tooth." It's the rule that keeps our courts full and our grudges deep. We live in a "you scratch my back, and I'll scratch yours" world. We've embraced this philosophy in every relationship. Whether at work, school, church, home, or in the neighborhood, we look for fair and equal treatment; we want to get back as much as we give. Moreover, we don't want to give one ounce more than others give.

Coming to Grips: I Am a Back-scratcher too

I pastored for many years, and this reality always frustrated me. I watched good men and women go through stressful days and turn into self-absorbed, resource-hoarding, finger-pointing whiners. "Why doesn't someone else show up to help? Am I the only one who cares? If nobody else is going to step up, I'm going to quit too!"

I couldn't believe it. Many times I wanted to scream. "I'm tired too! Nobody cares about whether or not I've worked eighty hours. Quit whining!" I couldn't see my own back-scratching mentality. I was frustrated because I was convinced I was giving more than the rest, and they didn't care. This wasn't fair. If I was going to scratch their backs, they needed to scratch mine.

This frustration over the lack of generosity in the majority of churchgoers was a daily part of ministry. You may have heard that twenty percent of the people do eighty percent of the work and give eighty percent of the money. In fact, in my consulting with churches, I am thrilled when churches reach such a level of generosity that thirty or thirty-five percent of the people carry the load. That means the number of people doing nothing in the church has reduced from eighty percent to sixty-five or seventy percent. Even that sounds frustrating, doesn't it? It was driving me crazy. I was working hard; why shouldn't the rest of them? It wasn't fair!

Years later, after leaving pastoral ministry, I found myself as one of the twenty percent in my local church. I was driving home late one night from a consulting job a hundred miles from home. I was exhausted from working a full time job, consulting on the side, and filling many roles at church. After all, there were plenty of other people who could do half the things I was killing myself to complete. I had been exhausted the last Sunday and had found out some church folks had been grumbling over the fact I stayed home from church. I was honestly so tired that I just needed a day to rest, and that doesn't happen for me at church.

Their lack of gratitude and accusations were more than I could take. In my heart I was yelling at God for making me be the one who had to be responsible. *Why don't they quit complaining and start helping? Don't they know I am doing ministry all week? I am only one person! I can't keep going like this. I've had it. They can find someone else to do this stuff. If they don't care, why should I?*

There are moments when God quietly waits for us to say something He can use to confront our sin. We assume the reason He is patiently listening is that He agrees with us. And then, once we have laid open our selfish attitude, He forces us to acknowledge that what we just said really is the way we think. We know it isn't okay, but we can't deny having said it. It is painful and exhilarating all at the same time. It is painful, because we have to confess our sin. It is exhilarating, because we know God is about to take us into one of those moments of transformation.

God's voice wasn't small or still. He was loud and clear. "You sound just like one of those whining churchgoers. What's that all about?" Immediately, my own words convicted me. I had already confessed my guilt. It was time to do some soul searching. *God why am I not willing to give? Why am I not generous with my time and my money? Why am I so limited in my willingness to sacrifice?*

You should never ask a question if you don't want the answer. God's voice became clear and I was arrested by His clarity. "You have never been generous. You have always operated out of a sense of reciprocity. You give just as much as you receive and you quit giving when you don't get back what you think you deserve. You're a back-scratcher!"

I don't know if the Holy Spirit speaks to you so sternly. But it left me undone. *You're right! I need you to help me change. I don't understand what a generous heart really is. If you'll teach me, I will listen.*

The next months proved to be a spiritual journey into the heart of a man who died on a cross and at the same time lavished mercy on those nearby (Luke 23:34). I came face to face with a friend who knew He was going to be deserted, yet encouraged Peter while confronting him (Matthew 26:31-32). I was undone by this man's willingness to reconcile long before his brother was willing to open the door and sit down at the family table (Revelation 3:20).

I am sorry God. All these years, I have limited my gifts to you by what others have been willing to give. I am not generous. I am a back-scratcher, and I need to wash my hands of this attitude. Help me to give like you gave. Help me serve out of respect for how you serve me.

In that prayer, I realized there is to be only one reciprocal relationship in my life. I am to love because He first loved me. I am to be holy because He is holy. I am to give of my life because He gave of His. No other person is to become the gauge by which I measure the fairness of my life.

His mercy was delivered to me when I didn't deserve it, so I am to lavish on others a generous portion of love, mercy, hope, forgiveness. I am to offer my first fruits. My gifts are to be pressed down, shaken together, running over. It doesn't matter if the people I serve deserve it. I don't give because they give. I give because He gave. The measuring stick—the only source of reciprocity—is Jesus. I give my life out of respect of His sacrificial love for me. That is generosity!

Jesus on Generosity

Jesus is calling us to walk away from a world that determines its willingness to give to others based on fairness. However, we are so engrained in the back-scratching mentality of this world that we have a hard time understanding when He calls us to respond to injustice with generosity rather than our right to repayment—reciprocity.

> You have heard that it was said, "Eye for eye, and tooth for tooth." But I tell you, Do not resist an evil person. If someone strikes you on the right cheek, turn to him the other also. And if someone wants to sue you and take your tunic, let him have your cloak as well. If someone forces you to go one mile, go with him two miles. Give to the one who asks you, and do not turn away from the one who wants to borrow from you. —Matthew 5:38-42

Now, here we are, face to face with Jesus, and like my children, we want to cry, "That's not fair!" We resist the apparent injustice being inflicted on us. We know that when someone strikes us on the cheek we have the right to fight back or be paid for our injury. When someone forces us to help him or her, like the Roman soldiers could force a person to carry their pack one mile, we understand that we should only have to do what the law requires. It is unfair to begin with, so why would we go beyond the letter of the law? When someone steals from us, why would we ignore the offense and find a way to meet that person's need?

When we evaluate Jesus' statement from our back-scratchers worldview, none of it makes sense. However, Jesus turned the whole equation on its end. His sacrifice on the cross shows us the heart of the Heavenly Father. He is not one who treats us as we deserve. He offered grace and forgiveness, not because we had given Him something equal to His sacrifice, but because He loved us so much He was willing to take our punishment. He didn't just give us just enough love to help us feel better. He didn't limit His love by what we deserve. He lavished His love on us (1 John 3:1) and then called us to take the cloth, follow His example, and start washing feet (John 13:4-5). In fact, Jesus' reason for calling us to this level of generosity is that we are to reflect the character of God.

You have heard that it was said, "Love your neighbor and hate your enemy." But I tell you: Love your enemies and pray for those who persecute you, that you may be sons of your Father in heaven. He causes his sun to rise on the evil and the good, and sends rain on the righteous and the unrighteous. If you love those who love you, what reward will you get? Are not even the tax collectors doing that? And if you greet only your brothers, what are you doing more than others? Do not even pagans do that? Be perfect, therefore, as your heavenly Father is perfect. — Matthew 5:43-48

I turn the other cheek, offer my coat, walk the extra mile, and love my enemy because I want to reflect the perfect nature of God.

If we are going to have hearts that reflect the character of Christ, we have to come to grips with the reality that our level of investment in those around us cannot be determined by what is fair. In fact, it has nothing to do with fairness. It has everything to do with an appropriate response to grace—generous expressions of gratitude. It has everything to do with living out the kind of love Christ displayed for us. It was a *lavished* love— a generous portion.

It isn't fair grace, but unfair grace. This inequity is the power of grace. It isn't restricted by the actions of the offender. It is empowered by Christ's mercy. It isn't limited by our sense of injustice. It is unbridled as we reflect the Father's grace.

If I am to be like Jesus, I am to generously pour my life into others as an act of unbridled grace. I am not to take on the mentality of a back-scratcher, which is "I'll give when I'm given to, and in equal measure."

I will look at the cross, see the overwhelming love and self-sacrifice of someone else paying for my sin, and embrace its call to a life that imitates that kind of generosity.

We limit what God can do through us when we refuse to give as Jesus gave. History is full of men and women of faith who sacrificed what others wouldn't in order for God to accomplish what man could not: Martin Luther King Jr., Billy Graham, and Mother Teresa—the big names are recognizable. But, there are hundreds of thousands of faithful believers who have been transformed by the lavished love of God who sacrificially invest themselves in ways that make a significant impact on the lives of those around them. You and I are called to open ourselves up to the possibility that God might just change someone's life because we choose generosity over back-scratching.

We can never fully understand the love of the cross until we give up the right to receive as much as we give. We are called to "live a life of love just as Christ loved us." He gave himself up for us. There was no limit. His love was *lavished*.

Generosity in Reconciliation

We are called to be imitators of God as dearly loved children (Ephesians 5). Paul described this as a ministry of *reconciliation* (2 Corinthians 5:18-21). Jesus calls the church to repent by referring to a reconciliation pattern illustrated by sitting down at the same table (Revelation 3:20).

In a world where relationships are falling apart in staggering numbers, we need to embrace generosity in reconciliation. We are to be the first to the table, consistently declaring our willingness to work through the issues that will bring healing. Reconciliation goes beyond forgiveness. Forgiveness is something we give, but doesn't necessarily dictate that we stay close to the one we forgave. Reconciliation is something we work at. Reconciliation calls for a renewed relationship and implies a process where we find healing from the sins that separate us. While we explore this in more depth in another chapter, it is important to understand that we cannot reflect the generous love of the Father while maintaining an unwillingness to find healing in our relationships.

Generosity Changes Our Relationships

When we choose this kind of generosity, it changes how we deal with our relationships. It changes our relationship with our spouse and children. It changes our approach to reconciliation. It changes how we handle church, and it changes how we interact with the world around us. In the chapters to come we will explore what each of these relationships can become when we embrace God's call to turn the other cheek, walk the extra mile, and care more about the needs of our brother and sister than the offense that could separate us. We will choose to walk away from a back-scratcher world, refuse to evaluate our lives through a filter of fairness, and live the generous love of Christ.

Hand Soap for Back-scratchers

"Wash your hands, you sinners, and purify your hearts, you double-minded" (James 4:8). We live in a world that doesn't understand the generous grace of the Father. However, we are to embrace it. We must take an honest assessment of our willingness to give as He gave. We live in a back-scratcher world, and it is time to wash our hands of a value system that will only give to the level it has received. We are to treat our neighbors as we want to be treated, not as they have treated us.

As you explore the pages of this book, it is my prayer that God will empower you to love as He loves and give as He gives—generously.

2

ONE OBLIGATION

ॐ

The Upside Down Golden Rule

I was driving home from work and enjoying my daily dose of talk radio. The conversation had turned to local injustice, and the callers were venting their frustration. One gentleman exclaimed, "Why don't people just follow the Golden Rule? I mean, I have the right to be treated the same way they would want to be treated, right?"

I chuckled at His comment. It illustrates how we want to read Jesus' teachings. We love the rules of fairness as long as they are calling someone else to sacrifice. But when our back isn't going to be scratched at the same level we are expected to help others, we quickly abandon a commitment to this servant principle. Like this caller, we take a principle that calls us to embrace generosity and turn it on its end. "They owe me. They have to treat me fairly! God said so!"

It reminds me of a morning when my wife and I both woke up grumpy. We were doing our best to not bark at each other, but it wasn't working very well. I said something to her with a less-than-kind attitude (after all she was doing the same). She shot back, "You need to treat me nice!"

"Why? You aren't," was my quick response. My reciprocity was in full swing.

Her response brought us both to laughter, but illustrates our tendency to miss the point of the Golden Rule. She said, "Well, you can treat me nice, even if I'm not treating you nice!"

When we read the Golden Rule and begin evaluating how others should change their actions toward us, we are actually filtering Jesus' call to selflessness through our selfishness. It is difficult to see the truth of Jesus' call to a generous spirit when all we keep asking is "What's in it for me?"

We want reciprocity, but only when we are the one who is owed something. We demand fairness as long as we are not the one of whom it is demanded. However, we must lock eyes with Jesus, who died on the cross for our sin and then called us to serve as He serves. We have to come to grips with the fact that He has ended all other sources of reciprocity in our lives. We can no longer judge fairness based on how others treat us. Our sense of justice is determined by God's grace toward us.

God Determines What's Fair

In this chapter and the next we are going to look at a parable that illustrates Christ's call to embrace God as our only obligation. He speaks of a vineyard owner whose workers accused him of treating them unfairly. Read how Jesus tries to move us away from hearts committed to equal treatment:

> For the kingdom of heaven is like a landowner who went out early in the morning to hire men to work in his vineyard. He agreed to pay them a denarius for the day and sent them into his vineyard. About the third hour he

went out and saw others standing in the marketplace doing nothing. He told them, "You also go and work in my vineyard, and I will pay you whatever is right." So they went. He went out again about the sixth hour and the ninth hour and did the same thing. About the eleventh hour he went out and found still others standing around. He asked them, "Why have you been standing here all day long doing nothing?" "Because no one has hired us," they answered. He said to them, "You also go and work in my vineyard." When evening came, the owner of the vineyard said to his foreman, "Call the workers and pay them their wages, beginning with the last ones hired and going on to the first." The workers who were hired about the eleventh hour came and each received a denarius. So when those came who were hired first, they expected to receive more. But each one of them also received a denarius. When they received it, they began to grumble against the landowner. "These men who were hired last worked only one hour," they said, "and you have made them equal to us who have borne the burden of the work and the heat of the day." But he answered one of them, "Friend, I am not being unfair to you. Didn't you agree to work for a denarius? Take your pay and go. I want to give the man who was hired last the same as I gave you. Don't I have the right to do what I want with my own money? Or are you envious because I am generous?" —Matthew 20:1-15

The landowner is God, and we are the vineyard workers. The workers evaluated God's character by comparing their blessings to that of their coworkers. Their lack of generosity colored their understanding of the situation. This wasn't about God and His desire to lavish grace. This was about their paycheck and feeling as if they had not received equal treatment. They were back-scratchers, and they knew an unfair deal when they saw one. They worked longer than these latecomers and were owed a greater reward. They accused God of being unfair.

Before we get too proud and point fingers at their sin, we need to take a long, hard look at our relationships. We do the same thing. We claim our right to make decisions at home, church, and work based on how much longer we've been around than those who are trying to tell us their wishes. We stake our claim as the boss, and nobody gets to tell us what will and won't be. We sacrificed more than the rest, and we deserve special treatment. Too many times, we stand with these workers and try to claim a special standing because of the length of our service or the depth of our sacrifice.

God stops the workers in their tracks. He lets them know that He has the right to express His generosity however He chooses. This is about His goodness, His generous character as a holy God. He gives because that is the kind of God He is.

God fulfilled His promise to the complainers. They received the reward He promised. Their sense of injustice was warped by their desire for fair treatment.

God is not about to subject himself to their comparison. The workers' accusation flowed from a value system that demanded payment based on work, not generosity. In their minds, fairness should be determined by what a person deserves. God is not going to allow this. He rewards out of His grace, not because we are worthy, or as repayment for services rendered. He sets the standard of what is fair. Like the workers, we tend to embrace a standard God has not authorized—reciprocity.

There is one source of fairness, one source of reciprocity, one reciprocal relationship—our relationship to God. Moreover, in that relationship, we are the ones who have been treated better than we deserve. We are the ones obligated to reciprocate—to give because we have been given to.

The justice Christ provides is not a justice based on the laws of fair treatment. The justice we are given is an act of generous grace. And that model, that one relationship of reciprocity, must change every other relationship.

I am obligated to live a spirit-empowered life of love that models the sacrificial generosity of Christ. I reciprocate God's love by showing others the same mercy and love He lavished on me. I must not limit the love I show, but *lavish* it, regardless of anyone's worthiness. This is the only kind of reciprocity I can embrace.

Nobody is obligated to me because of my goodness toward him or her. My generosity flows from my obligation to Christ. To hold onto my right to demand equal treatment from others, just because I gave them more than they gave me, is a slap in God's face. I cannot accept the forgiveness of my great debt and then hold tightly to another's debt to me. This one reciprocal relationship holds me accountable to grace.

Without Excuse

This one reciprocal relationship leaves us without excuse. Forgiveness can never be withheld—we are obligated to give it.

Trust is another matter—that is always earned. However, the willingness to deal with whatever separates us from our brother is the spirit of reconciliation that Christ modeled and demands we embrace.

Reciprocity can be understood as an obligation to return the favor. Because I treated my wife well, she is obligated to treat me well. Because I sacrifice for my children, they are obligated to show me respect. Because I work hard, my employer is obligated to give me a raise. Because I sacrifice for the church, they are obligated to give me recognition.

We live with these expectations every day. However, Jesus has established the only reciprocal relationship we are to embrace. And in this relationship with Jesus, He is the one who gave. We received. That obligates us to a response.

The Obligation: Spirit-empowered Generosity

Paul declares the only fair response to God's generous gift of grace.

> Therefore, brothers, we have an obligation—but it is not to the sinful nature, to live according to it. For if you live according to the sinful nature, you will die; but if by the Spirit you put to death the misdeeds of the body, you will live, because those who are led by the Spirit of God are sons of God. —Romans 8:12

We have one obligation; we are to live by the power of the Spirit. We are not to indulge in the selfish tendencies of our hearts. We are sons and daughters of the God who generously gave His son to die in our place. That one act of undeserved grace leaves us with an absolute call to abandon our demand to be treated fairly and embrace the generosity that allows us to give like Jesus gave.

Paul talks about this in Ephesians 5 when he calls us to "Live a life of love, just as Christ loved us and gave himself up for us as a fragrant offering and sacrifice to God" (v. 2). Christ's sacrificial generosity established our model for investing in others.

While we are going to explore the teachings on generosity in relationships in later chapters, it is important to note the impact of choosing this kind of generosity. When each person in the relationship shows generosity, with gratitude and reverence toward Christ, everyone's needs are met without manipulation. When I give with no expectation of a return gift, always keeping the needs of the other person as my focus, and they do the same, there is a fulfillment that cannot be manufactured. The Holy Spirit brings unity into relationships when reciprocity is replaced by generosity.

Paul takes the principle further. In 1 Corinthians 6:19-20 he reminds us that the reason we are to be careful in our relationship with the opposite sex is that our bodies are not our own—we were bought at a price. My obligation isn't just to the person with whom I have a relationship. I am obligated to honor God.

Jesus gives us a picture of this obligation to the father in the story of the prodigal son (Luke 15:11-32). The son comes home and surrenders his right to demand special treatment. The amazing picture of God's generosity is displayed in the Father's response. Even though the son's guilt is unquestioned, the father lavishes mercy and grace. The son is embraced, and his full status as a son is restored. Reconciliation pours from the father's generous grace. Even when the older brother complains at the unfair treatment he feels he has received, the father reminds him that he should evaluate his circumstances in light of the father's ever-present generosity, not the brother's unworthiness.

Rearranged Rights

Our obligation to the Father is tough. It demands that we offer more grace and mercy than people deserve. It demands that our behavior reflect the Father's heart. When those who should care for us most hurt us, this obligation to generously lavish mercy seems unfair. The only way we can find the grace to follow Christ's pattern is to once again remind ourselves of the demand His mercy places on us.

Peter was struggling with this issue, and Jesus puts it plainly: your obligation to this kind of generous grace is serious.

Then Peter came to Jesus and asked, "Lord, how many times shall I forgive my brother when he sins against me? Up to seven times?" Jesus answered, "I tell you, not seven times, but seventy-seven times. "Therefore, the kingdom of heaven is like a king who wanted to settle accounts with his servants. As he began the settlement, a man who owed him ten thousand talents was brought to him. Since he was not able to pay, the master ordered that he and his wife and his children and all that he had be sold to repay the debt. The servant fell on his knees before him. "Be patient with me," he begged, "and I will pay back everything." The servant's master took pity on him, canceled the debt and let him go. But when that servant went out, he found one of his fellow servants who owed him a hundred denarii. He grabbed him and began to choke him. "Pay back what you owe me!" he demanded. His fellow servant fell to his knees and begged him, "Be patient with me, and I will pay you back." But he refused. Instead, he went off and had the man thrown into prison until he could pay the debt. When the other servants saw what had happened, they were greatly distressed and went and told their master everything that had happened. Then the master called the servant in. "You wicked servant," he said, "I canceled all that debt of yours because you begged me to. Shouldn't you have had mercy on your fellow servant just as I had on you?" In anger his master turned him over to the jailers to be tortured, until he should pay back all he owed. "This is how my heavenly Father will treat each of you unless you forgive your brother from your heart." —Matthew 18:21-35

Our obligation to God is concrete. He forgave me when I didn't deserve it, and that must change my attitude toward those who owe me. Jesus reminds us that God will hold us accountable for our response. I might be legally justified in holding someone to his or her obligation to me. I might be morally justified in demanding my spouse reciprocate my sacrifice for the family. They owe me, and I have a right to repayment. But, Jesus reminds us that His sacrifice on the cross rearranges our rights. We are now obligated to reflect His generosity.

I am sure to be hurt by those close to me. I must forgive their debt. I am sure to be abandoned by those who swore to protect me. I must forgive their debt. I am sure to give more than I receive. I must forgive the debt. Why? Because that is what Jesus did for me.

Transformed by Lavished Love

Jesus wants the love He lavished on me to transform how I deal with the injustices I face. I am to be as generous with others as God has been with me.

Dear friends, let us love one another, for love comes from God. Everyone who loves has been born of God and knows God. Whoever does not love does not know God, because God is love. This is how God showed his love among us: He sent his one and only Son into the world that we might live through him. This is love: not that we loved God, but that he loved us and sent his Son as an atoning sacrifice for our sins. Dear friends, since God so loved us, we also ought to love one another. . . . We love because he first loved us. —1 John 4:7-11, 19

I don't love my enemy because he deserves it. I don't love my children because they have earned it. I don't love my spouse because she will return the favor. I don't love my neighbor because he did something for me and I owe him.

I love because Christ loved me. It was His ultimate and absolute act of generosity that obligates me to reflect the holiness of God through my generous response to those I feel owe me something.

A good pastor friend of mine went through the painful experience of being confronted by God over this very issue. I'll call him John to protect his identity. He was young in ministry and was pastoring a church with a history of backbiting. That kind of church is a tough assignment for even a seasoned leader. John was young in ministry, and he was getting eaten alive.

As soon as new families began attending, they were pulled aside by these backbiters and got an earful about how awful Pastor John was.

If you've ever been attacked in such a horrific way, you understand that emotions can run deep. It is difficult to know what to do when you are wounded and your heart is broken. It is moments like this that following Jesus' teaching to lavish kindness and mercy on the enemy isn't our natural response.

John wasn't going to allow these people to ruin his reputation, so he decided it was time to take control. John got to new families before his enemies could. Guests arrived and the pastor quickly warned them to be careful of these gossips. John let the guests know that these evil people would try to turn new families against him.

He was trying to protect his reputation and give himself a chance to begin relationships with these new families. However, John was choosing a method of conflict resolution that ignored Jesus' teaching to pour kindness on our enemies. Paul said this kind of generosity pours coals of shame on their heads (Romans 12:20). The picture is reminiscent of the coals that purified Isaiah (Isaiah 6:6). This isn't a scripture that teaches us a backhanded game of revenge. God uses our kindness to bring cleansing to our enemies. Kindness as a response to an attack brings a transformation of our enemy's heart.

But that was not how John was dealing with his pain. He was throwing more division onto the situation, and God was not being honored. He was fighting fire with fire, and everyone was getting burned.

It got so bad that John and his parishioners would see each other in the grocery and intentionally duck into aisles to avoid each other. Both the pastor and his people had missed the point. God's character demands that we embrace a form of reconciliation bathed in a generous portion of grace. Something had to change, and God was going to teach John a lesson in the process.

A church member who had become one of John's enemies became deathly ill. *Should I visit him in the hospital or just avoid the conflict all together?* The thought stung John's heart. He knew the answer, but was face to face with the reality that behaving like Christ and maintaining his back-scratcher cry of "You apologize first!" could no longer coexist. John was going to have to choose to show extravagant grace or hold to his "eye for an eye" right to fight.

The Holy Spirit broke his stubborn hold to justice, and he ministered to this hurting family. His kindness, his generous imitation of the life of Christ who gave himself up for us before we ever sought his forgiveness, became the tool God used to heal the wounds. John had embraced his reciprocity to Christ and loved these people as Christ loved him.

In the end, the humility he learned and the relationships God healed were part of the blessing John took away from the experience. Something powerful happens when we quit responding to conflict out of a sense of justice and start modeling the love of Christ. Transformation comes to our enemies as well as to us.

Generous Grace Becomes Generous Worship

I am able to show such great sacrifice only when I keep a strong sense of just how much Christ sacrificed for me. In Luke 7:36-48, a lady with a very sinful past weeps and pours perfume on Jesus' feet. The Pharisee who owned the house where Jesus was staying, a man named Simon, is appalled that Jesus would allow such a sinful person to go on like this. Knowing his heart, Jesus asks Simon a penetrating question.

"Two men owed money to a certain moneylender. One owed him five hundred denarii, and the other fifty. Neither of them had the money to pay him back, so he canceled the debts of both. Now which of them will love him more?" Simon replied, "I suppose the one who had the bigger debt canceled." "You have judged correctly," Jesus said. —Luke 7:41-42

Jesus reminds Simon that this woman's generous worship flows from a heart that has been forgiven much. Then Jesus confronts Simon with the truth. "But he who has been forgiven little loves little" (Luke 7:47).

When we don't take our sin seriously, or we have forgotten just how great a sacrifice Christ made on our behalf, we lose our willingness to generously invest ourselves in service to God. In our arrogance we start weighing the costs and benefits, and determine our level of investment based on the expected return.

However, when we look at Christ's sacrifice and embrace a sense of reverence for what He did, the Holy Spirit empowers our ability to heal broken relationships. He brings deep fulfillment as we serve our families and our church. He enables us to make a difference in the world around us. Where once we weighed the fairness of every issue in every relationship, now we look at the inequity of Christ's sacrifice and quit looking for repayment from others.

Crushing the "Fairness Scale"

The cross crushes our "fairness scale" and makes it irrelevant to our willingness to serve. Whether or not the benefits outweigh the sacrifice is no longer the issue. When Christ calls us to serve, it is fair. When He calls us to forgive, it is fair. When He calls us to sacrifice, it is fair. His sacrifice has determined what is fair. Our investment can never outweigh His generosity.

> This is how we know what love is: Jesus Christ laid down his life for us. And we ought to lay down our lives for our brothers. —1 John 3:16

Our sacrifice is not to be a response to any other person's behavior. It is to be an act of sacrificial generosity that reflects the character of Christ. God's generous love obligates us to imitate His character. He is my measuring stick—my one reciprocal relationship. He laid down His life for me, and out of reverence for His gift, I am to generously serve.

3
TRANSFORMATIONAL GENEROSITY

∽

It's God's Character

There have been moments when I have watched my children respond with a lack of grace and realized they are imitating me. As much as I want them to learn the generous spirit of Christ, I am guilty of falling to my own selfish tendencies. It breaks my heart when what flows out of my heart doesn't reflect the character of God. That is why I must pay attention to this call to reflect the generosity of God. It is a core part of who He is. And He wants me to look like Him—to be holy as He is holy.

Jesus goes so far as to declare generosity as God's motivation for our salvation. In Matthew 20, we revisit the parable of the vineyard owner. As you remember from the last chapter, the vineyard owner represents God, and we are the workers He has hired. The vineyard owner hired some workers early in the day, others at mid-day, and others just before he returned to pay them their wages.

The workers who were hired early in the day were offended that the vineyard owner chose to reward everyone with the same pay regardless of how long he had been on the crew. This is the picture of our salvation and eternal reward. Some join God's family early in life, others midway through, and still others late in the day. This is a powerful reality about God's mercy toward us. It's based in His character, not the length of our service.

While pastoring in South Dakota, I had the pleasure of leading Don to the Lord on the last night of his life. He was lying in a hospital bed, barely able to communicate. "Don, do you want to ask Jesus into your heart? Squeeze my finger if you do." His weak squeeze was an act of faith. "I'm going to pray, and you pray in your heart and tell Jesus you want Him to forgive you. Squeeze my finger if you understand." He tightened his grip.

I prayed. Don prayed. He entered the vineyard late in the day, but the vineyard owner honored Don's heart. The next day he slipped into eternity and enjoyed the same reward he would have received had he accepted Christ as a little boy.

To those who rejoice in the reality that a place in the Kingdom isn't earned, this thought brings joy. But, to those who measure all of life, even grace, by what is fair and what isn't, this injustice cannot be tolerated.

That is what was wrong with the workers in Jesus' parable. Why did they accuse God of being unfair? They didn't reflect God's character. Listen to Jesus' words as He describes the Father's motivation for delivering grace.

> Am I not allowed to do what I choose with what belongs to me? Or do you begrudge my generosity? — Matthew 20:15)

Our very salvation flows out of this character trait of God— He is generous. In fact, His character defines generosity. Jesus uses the same word that is translated "generosity" when He is called *good teacher*. As He deals with a young man who is lacking this core character trait of the Father, He points out how difficult it is for us to embrace godly generosity, or goodness.

As Jesus was starting out on his way to Jerusalem, a man came running up to him, knelt down, and asked, "Good Teacher, what must I do to inherit eternal life?"

"Why do you call me good?" Jesus asked. "Only God is truly good. But to answer your question, you know the commandments: 'You must not murder. You must not commit adultery. You must not steal. You must not testify falsely. You must not cheat anyone. Honor your father and mother.'"

"Teacher," the man replied, "I've obeyed all these commandments since I was young."

Looking at the man, Jesus felt genuine love for him. "There is still one thing you haven't done," he told him. "Go and sell all your possessions and give the money to the poor, and you will have treasure in heaven. Then come, follow me."

At this the man's face fell, and he went away sad, for he had many possessions.

Jesus looked around and said to his disciples, "How hard it is for the rich to enter the Kingdom of God!" This amazed them. But Jesus said again, "Dear children, it is very hard to enter the Kingdom of God. In fact, it is easier for a camel to go through the eye of a needle than for a rich person to enter the Kingdom of God!"

The disciples were astounded. "Then who in the world can be saved?" they asked.

Jesus looked at them intently and said, "Humanly speaking, it is impossible. But not with God. Everything is possible with God." —Mark 10:17-26 NLT

The word translated *good,* in verses 17 and 18, is the same word Jesus used to talk about generosity in the parable of the vineyard owner. This generosity is not simply an act of good will. The Romans used this term to refer to the generous character of a person who is expected to give back to society. (*Dictionary of Jesus and the Gospels* (58), Joel Green, Scott McKnight, and I. Howard Marshall, InterVarsity Press)

The rich young ruler assumed that Jesus was just another morally good man. He owed society something and should therefore give back. But Jesus wanted to show that the kind of generous character that flows from God's heart cannot be compared to the back-scratching displays of limited generosity embraced by men. The goodness of God, His generosity, is the character of one who lavishes mercy, love, and grace on those around him. That is the goodness that flows from the Heavenly Father's heart. It is the core of His character that drove Him to offer His son as our sacrifice.

Where we tend to consider generosity as a single act of giving something up, Jesus is telling us that true generosity is the ongoing character of goodness. We don't give of ourselves because it is convenient, or out of the acknowledgement that this sacrifice is a temporary inconvenience that will soon end. No, this goodness is an intentional pouring out of our lives so that others can find transformation through Christ.

Jesus warns us that only God is truly that generous. In fact, Jesus says, "Humanly speaking, it is impossible" (v. 27). This kind of pouring out of ourselves is not natural for us. Our spirits are not generous but selfish. Only as the Holy Spirit unleashes God's character in us can we find the transformation necessary to reflect the character of God—to give as He gives. "But not with God. Everything is possible with God" (Mark 10:27 NLT).

This young man was spiritually defeated because he couldn't embrace a godly character. He could not bring himself to sacrifice for others' needs. Legalism was easy, but godly character was more than he could give. There was no paycheck to justify the sacrifice.

True generosity isn't about the money. It's about the heart. When the heart reflects the character of God, we give generously of our time, our energy, our money, our emotions. God looks at our willingness to serve others and once again declares, "It is good." When our hearts reflect the image of fallen man, godly goodness is gone and generosity is impossible.

It's a Spiritual Fruit

Paul understood this. Selfishness is the byproduct of our natural spiritual condition. We are born with the impact of Adam's sin ruling the way we think and act (Romans 8:5). We want what we want. We are selfish, so we behave selfishly, not generously. Paul calls it the "works of the flesh" (Galatians 5).

However, when the spirit controls the way we think, when we are being transformed by the renewing of our minds (Romans 12:1-2), God's character flows out of us. Paul calls this "the fruit of the Spirit" (Galatians 5). It is an interesting list: love, joy, peace, patience, kindness, goodness, faithfulness, gentleness, and self-control. There in the middle, where we normally skim the surface, lies the very word Jesus uses to define this generous heart of God—*goodness*—or a character of generosity. We experience the restoration of His goodness that lavishes love on us, whether we deserve it or not.

This goodness is generosity on steroids. It is deeper than a one-time action. It is the character of generosity. It isn't choosing to give a little extra in the offering because the pastor is watching. It isn't ignoring our children's bad behavior because we are too tired to fight them. It isn't helping with the dishes so we don't have to listen to our spouse complain. It is the deep-down character trait of a giving heart that flows freely from an unselfish spirit.

Transformation Needed

This "goodness on steroids" isn't something we can manufacture. It flows from the Holy Spirit's activity in our hearts and minds. We are able to experience this kind of generosity when the Holy Spirit is flowing in us. Only then can our responses reflect His goodness, His generous grace.

We can produce a generous act from time to time, but if our character is to reflect the character of God, then the Holy Spirit must deliver the ability to lavish love and mercy as Jesus did. He was generous when it didn't profit Him. He was generous when we didn't deserve it. He was generous when it cost Him far more than He could afford. To live out that kind of generosity takes a transformation of our hearts and minds.

Paul talks about this transformation in Romans 12 when he writes.

> I appeal to you therefore, brothers, by the mercies of God, to present your bodies as a living sacrifice, holy and acceptable to God, which is your spiritual worship. Do not be conformed to this world, but be transformed by the renewal of your mind, that by testing you may discern what is the will of God, what is good and acceptable and perfect. —Romans 12:1-2 ESV

Paul calls us to offer our bodies as living sacrifices and then defines that as "holy and acceptable." It is holy because it reflects the very character of God. He gave himself for our salvation. He was our sacrifice; it was His generous act of mercy. In view of that act of mercy, we are called to live this life as an act of giving of ourselves. The result is a mind that is transformed so that it understands the heart of God.

When we choose to give of ourselves as Christ gave, we understand the "good" will of God (v. 2). Yes, it is the same word—generous. We know his character because it flows in our hearts. His generous grace transforms our selfishness so that we can truly worship—we generously give of ourselves.

When we have experienced this transformational generosity, our thinking changes. We treat people differently than we did before. We give, rather than take. We ask, "How can I serve my spouse, my kids, my church, my world?"

It isn't natural. It is the result of the Holy Spirit's transformational grace generously poured out in my heart. When God generously transforms my heart, my relationships are also transformed. This is the beauty and power of grace and love when it is lavished on us. It causes us to lavish the same grace and love on others. We are finally capable of imitating the agape love of God.

Imitating a Generous God

Paul lays out the issue in Ephesians 5. While we are going to study this scripture's implication for family life in the next few chapters, we must understand the fundamental issue: we are to imitate the character of Christ in our relationships at home, at church, and in the world. Listen to Paul's words as he helps us understand that our generosity is to be a reflection of God's character.

Be imitators of God, therefore, as dearly loved children and live a life of love, just as Christ loved us and gave himself up for us as a fragrant offering and sacrifice to God. But among you there must not be even a hint of sexual immorality, or of any kind of impurity, or of greed, because these are improper for God's holy people. Nor should there be obscenity, foolish talk or coarse joking, which are out of place, but rather thanksgiving. For of this you can be sure: No immoral, impure or greedy person—such a man is an idolater—has any inheritance in the kingdom of Christ and of God. Let no one deceive you with empty words, for because of such things God's wrath comes on those who are disobedient. Therefore do not be partners with them. For you were once darkness, but now you are light in the Lord. Live as children of light (for the fruit of the light consists in all goodness, righteousness and truth). . . . Do not get drunk on wine, which leads to debauchery. Instead, be filled with the Spirit. Speak to one another with psalms, hymns and spiritual songs. Sing and make music in your heart to the Lord, always giving thanks to God the Father for everything, in the name of our Lord Jesus Christ. Submit to one another out of reverence for Christ. —Ephesians 5:1-9, 18-21

Paul addresses us as ones who have been transformed by the lavished love of God. Paul calls us "dearly loved children" (Ephesians 5:1). The word is formed from the word for unconditional love—*agape*. He uses it in a way that communicates that God's love is now a part of our character. In essence he is saying, "as children who have been so loved by God that you now reflect his agape love in your hearts, be just like God" (author's paraphrase). The very reason I can even begin to think about reflecting the generous love of God is that He has transformed me. But, since that is true, imitating God is no longer an option. It is a command.

How do I imitate His generous grace? I "live a life of love" that resembles the sacrificial model of Christ. He "gave himself up for me as a fragrant offering and sacrifice to God" (Ephesians 5:2). That will have an impact on my sexuality, my thinking, and how I handle my blessings. I am not to be greedy. Greed doesn't reflect the generous heart of God. I cannot tolerate that kind of darkness when the light of God has transformed me. That light is full of goodness—generosity. (Ephesians 5:8-9)

I can't keep responding to people out of a greedy spirit. That is idolatry, or self-worship. It isn't about my needs, my timetable, and my limited resources. It is about reflecting the image of the God who gave more of himself than I deserved. When I accept Him as my savior, and allow His love to transform my heart so much that I am now defined by His agape love, it must change how I handle my relationships. I must serve my brother "out of reverence for Christ" (Ephesians 5:21).

Paul goes on to explore this concept as it should be lived out at home, and we will explore the issue with him in coming chapters. But for now, we need to embrace God's call on our heart to look like Him.

Think about it. He left the safety and glory of heaven and made himself nothing for us. He put up with our insults and ridicule, and He still loved us. He let us beat Him to death and continued to pray on our behalf until He drew His last breathe. That kind of generosity transforms us when we let it change the way we think and act. That kind of generosity, when lived out in our relationships, transforms those around us.

It is no longer enough for us to look at God's character and marvel at His ability to sacrifice. He has given us the Holy Spirit to enable us to serve others with the same agape love. No, it isn't easy or natural. We are going to have to stay close to the Holy Spirit. He is going to have to give us the ability to continue giving when everything in us wants to call it quits. But, He delivered His generous mercy so that it could flow through us and transform others. As dearly loved children, transformed by the agape love of God, we are to be imitators of God—our "good" God, our "generous" God.

4
GENEROSITY IN MARRIAGE
PART I:
RESTORING EDEN

∽

Imagine a New Relationship

I doubt there is a single relationship in which the lack of generosity is so evident as in marriage. Moreover, there is no other relationship in which so much is to be gained by committing to end the back-scratching and demand for equal treatment.

We were created in absolute goodness, with an absolutely generous response to each other. We were made in God's image. As we will soon discover, men and women no longer reflect God's generous character. In fact, we are deeply committed to the effect of the curse; we fight to be boss. The hyper-competitiveness demands reciprocity rather than Christlike service.

Can you even begin to imagine what our families would be like if each of us put the other person's needs before our own? A husband comes home exhausted from work, looks at his wife, who is obviously as tired as he is, and asks, "What would you like me to cook for dinner?" A son or daughter comes home, finishes his or her homework, and then does the dishes, aware of the sacrifice Mom and Dad are making to provide for the family. A brother or sister gives up the comfy spot on the couch so that a sibling has a place to sit. Yes, it sounds like utopia, and we rarely experience this kind of generosity in family relationships on a regular basis, but I believe the Holy Spirit wants to enable a generous spirit in us to such an extent that these behaviors are regularly experienced.

While a spirit of helping others is supposed to be a natural response in families, people are not naturally generous at home. While we were created to reflect the goodness of God, Adam and Eve's sin destroyed God's character in humankind. Since that time to this, generosity isn't natural.

As we explore the scripture, it is vital that you recognize your emotional response to God's highest calling—to serve your spouse. It is likely that you will feel a certain level of rebellion against the idea that the place of serving is a place of blessing. For most of us, the position of serving feels like a position of weakness. I would suggest that the Holy Spirit wants to change our thinking so that we can once again experience the joy of waking up to God's precious gift of intimate friendship with our spouse.

What Happened to Eden?

In Genesis 2, we read an amazing story of God trying to bring absolute fulfillment into Adam's existence. It has always been amazing to me that God admitted He had not designed man to be completely fulfilled with God's company; he needed more. The Lord God said, "It is not good for the man to be alone. I will make a helper suitable for him" (v. 18). Man was walking with God in the cool of the garden, yet God said it wasn't good enough. God knew exactly what man needed—a helpmate. This would be someone to walk at his side as God's perfect fulfilling gift.

The Miracle Gift

God caused Adam to fall into a deep sleep and brought the miracle of woman to life from his side. Can you imagine her first thoughts upon waking up to life? *How did you bring me to life? You brought me to life out of Adam? He is the reason I exist? I will find fulfillment of my life's purpose when I pour myself into walking at his side, as his helpmate, his equal, his partner? You designed me as the perfect gift for him?*

Wow! He needs me! That must mean he is your greatest gift to me. As I learn his needs and hopes and dreams, I learn how you will use me to bring fulfillment to him. There is no other creature on the planet who can do what I was designed to do. I am God's greatest work, and he chose to use this partner of mine to be the source of my life. He is the head of the river, and I am the life-giving water that flows from the life God began in him.

Can you imagine Adam's response? It is an amazing moment. Adam and Eve awoke to the perfect gift from God. In their God-created perfection they served each other's needs in awe of the gift God had given them. They found fulfillment in their God-ordained position of helpmate.

Woman is God's best work. The animals, in all their amazing splendor, can't compare to what God did when He made woman. She is far and above the greatest gift ever given man. Man is woman's source of life. It is out of his side that

God brought her into existence. Her presence is more important to Adam than anything else God created.

Created to Serve—Obligated to God

To live generously in their marriage, both spouses should serve and love the other. God intended for Adam and Eve to find joy in meeting each other's needs. It was their joy because they were in dumbfounded awe of God's gift. Like a child with the perfect Christmas present, they protected and cherished each other with wide eyes and giddy spirits. It was *good*.

This is the point where our natural selves fight the idea that we were created to serve. Something in us rises up and says *I am more than that! I am my own person, not anyone's slave.* Don't misunderstand the point. Eve's identity isn't found in Adam. Adam's identity isn't found in Eve. Their identities are found in their relationship to God.

She is God's perfect gift; he is God's source of life for Eve. She isn't a "mini-me" for man to treat as a lesser being. He is responsible to God to care for her as the precious gift she is. Because God's purpose for her is to be a wonderful gift of love and fulfillment, she is not a slave. She is a helper. She is a gift from God like no other.

Neither is that to say that every person is called by God to marry. However, in the marriage relationship, both partners' roles are intended by God to be that of helpmates. She is God's perfect capstone to the creation, so she can find awe and respect of her relationship to God. God made her on purpose, because creation wasn't complete without her.

Adam recognizes this amazing gift and commits himself to serve her needs with everything in his soul. They were each wired to generously give of themselves to their partner without any concern for what they were receiving. They *served* each other.

Christlike, Not Conquered

One might be tempted to rise up and say "I am no one's servant!" We look at the position of serving, and our hearts resist it as a negative position. I would challenge you to reconsider the model of Christ; He didn't come to be served but to serve. Our fallen condition considers the place of servant as a place of mistreatment by believing that to serve is a sign of weakness or unfair treatment.

But Christ chose to serve; He wasn't forced. There is a vast difference between being conquered into submission and choosing to behave like Christ. The creation story is not a picture of slavery but of a fulfilled marriage where each person chooses to serve his or her spouse out of reverence for the Creator's heart.

Eve embraced her role alongside Adam, and Adam didn't force her to walk three steps behind him. Neither of them cared about ruling the roost. It wasn't in their thinking. God created them as equals who cared more about the other partner's needs than his or her own. They were both fulfilled without demanding or manipulating.

Enter Shame and Blame

Husband and wife were created to be equals without competition, shame, or blame. They were servants who cared more about the value of their partner than their own agenda. But that relationship radically changed as soon as sin destroyed God's character in them. Adam and Eve share a snack of forbidden fruit and everything changed. God's goodness was gone, and their generosity toward one another turned to selfishness.

God confronted their sin, and the change in their spirits was evident. Competition, shame, and blame became their first line of defense. They no longer were trying to protect each other; they were both trying to hang the blame on the other. Shame and blame became the fundamental expressions of the sinful heart as lived out in the marriage relationship. Listen to the shift.

> Then the eyes of both of them were opened, and they realized they were naked; so they sewed fig leaves together and made coverings for themselves. Then the man and his wife heard the sound of the Lord God as he was walking in the garden in the cool of the day, and they hid from the Lord God among the trees of the garden. But the Lord God called to the man, "Where are you?" He answered, "I heard you in the garden, and I was afraid because I was naked; so I hid." And he said, "Who told you that you were naked? Have you eaten from the tree that I commanded you not to eat from?" The man said, "The woman you put here with me—she gave me some fruit from the tree, and I ate it." —Genesis 3:7-12

The awe-filled love was gone. They had forgotten just how precious the gift of God had been. That gift (each other) was now the thing they blamed for their trouble. The curse was upon them, and they would now fight for dominance. Listen as God describes the impact of their sin. "Your desire will be for your husband, and he will rule over you" (Genesis 3:16).

God isn't saying the woman will have a constant sense of sexual desire for her husband; He is describing a fight for power. They are both going to want to rule the roost. She will want his power, and he will fight back to subdue her to his manipulative control. That isn't God's hope or desire—that is the effect of sinful people trying to live in the same space. The goodness of God—His generosity—is gone and is replaced by selfishness and a demanding spirit.

Not only was the "helper" approach to their marriage destroyed, God was no longer the hinge pin of their relationship. Rather than run to Him, they ran away from Him. The friendship with God that had been the glue of their awe-filled love, was now defined by fear and hiding.

Here's the point: we were created to serve each other. We were created as equal partners, perfectly designed as God's greatest gift to one another. No shame, no blame, just an honest desire to meet the needs of the other. Sin destroyed that generous character of God and replaced it with a self-centered, back-scratching mentality that uses shame and blame to get what we want when we want it. God's character, His generous lavishing of love, is not natural for us. While we're intended to look like Him, we now are full of selfish ambition.

Imitate a Loving God

If we are going to experience the restoration of God's character—His goodness, His generosity—in our relationships, we are going to need the Holy Spirit to transform our hearts. That will change our relationship to our family.

That is exactly what Paul is referring to in Ephesians 5. He has just called to us to imitate God as dearly loved children by living a life of love. And then he defines what that looks like.

Submit to one another out of reverence for Christ. Wives, submit to your husbands as to the Lord. For the husband is the head of the wife as Christ is the head of the church, his body, of which he is the Savior. Now as the church submits to Christ, so also wives should submit to their husbands in everything. Husbands, love your wives, just as Christ loved the church and gave himself up for her to make her holy, cleansing her by the washing with water through the word, and to present her to himself as a radiant church, without stain or wrinkle or any other blemish, but holy and blameless. In this same way, husbands ought to love their wives as their own bodies. He who loves his wife loves himself. After all, no one ever hated his own body, but he feeds and cares for it, just as Christ does the church—for we are members of his body. "For this reason a man will leave his father and mother and be united to his wife, and the two will become one flesh." This is a profound mystery—but I am talking about Christ and the church. However, each one of you also must love his wife as he loves himself, and the wife must respect her husband. —Ephesians 5:21-33

When we approach this scripture from a back-scratcher mentality, we look for what Paul says we are entitled to receive. We read portions that weren't intended for us. Husbands say, "Ah hah! There it is. 'Wives, submit to your husband.' You must submit!" And wives say, "See, you are supposed to give up! You are supposed to sacrifice your needs for mine!"

I would kindly suggest we should all mind our own business. The instructions to wives were written to the wives. The instructions for the husbands were written to the husbands. If you want to find the one command that is intended for both, back up to verse 21. That one verse applies to everyone. In fact, it is the central command from which this entire discussion flows. "Submit to one another out of reverence for Christ."

In Awe of Christ

We are to choose to serve as Christ served—He gave himself up. It doesn't matter whether we are talking about our spouse, our children, our church, our school, our employer, or our neighbor. We have an obligation to imitate Christ, and that means we serve as He served. Period.

Why would we choose to do that?

There is only one reason. We are in awe of Christ's love for us. We look at Him and His sacrifice and we embrace the reality that He died so that the character of God could be restored in us. Where sin destroyed our ability to have healthy relationships, Christ died so God's generous love could once again dominate our relationships.

We cannot experience the sacrificial love of Christ and then act as if it has nothing to do with how we treat each other.

We are to look at Christ, and in reverence for His amazing love choose to serve others in the same way He served us.

That starts with husbands and wives. The demands made on husbands and wives in the verses following Ephesians 5:21 are not to be battering rams one spouse uses to force the other spouse to submit. In fact, the submission listed in verse 21 is a choice made by the person submitting. It isn't forced. The person being served doesn't demand it. It is a personal act of worship that flows from a heart that is in awe of God's miraculous gift—His sacrificial love.

The obligation, the reciprocity, is to Christ—not the spouse. We will serve the other because we revere Christ, not our spouse. God alone has the right to place a demand on our spouse. We are not God's enforcer. We have been commanded to serve, regardless of how our spouse responds to God's command.

As we look at Paul's instruction, neither partner is given the right to demand a certain behavior from his or her spouse. It is enough that God has demanded a certain behavior from us. What He demands of our spouse is none of our business.

Wives—Headwater Submission

Paul begins the description of submitting to one another out of reverence for Christ by reminding the wife that God brought her life out of man. He is the source, the headwaters, of her life. The wife is to submit to the husband out of the sense of awe and reverence she has for God's gift—her life. She is to submit to her husband as to the Lord because the husband is the "head" of her in the same way that Christ is the "head" of the church.

I loved this verse when I was a young married man. I remember one time, and only one time, trying it out. "You are supposed to submit to me!" The quirky smile on Diana's face let me know I had better get a far better understanding of this verse before I risk my life on it.

The word for *head* is not a word for hierarchy or authority. It refers to the beginning of something. It is used to describe the head of a river—its starting point. Paul is reminding the wife that the very source of her life was man's side. God gifted her with life through man, and out of reverence for that awe-filled gift, she is to fulfill her God-given purpose by serving his needs.

This is the call to come back to that amazing moment of waking up in the Garden and finding God smiling at us. He has brought her into existence as the perfect gift to her husband. She is God's pinnacle of creation—His perfect answer to man's need. She is not an object of subjection. She is to be something to her husband that God couldn't be. She is just like him—bone of his bones, and flesh of his flesh. And without her, he is "alone." (Genesis 2:18)

When she wakes up to the amazing purpose of God in her marriage and sees that to serve is not an act of lowering oneself but rising to her greatest calling, she can serve as Christ serves the church. Christ's act of unselfish generosity became the life from which we have all received God's blessing. When the wife serves her husband out of awe, love, and respect for the God who gave her life, transformation happens in man that cannot happen in any other way.

Through her partnership, her husband experiences God's full blessing. He knows he is valued because she serves him with a fervency that says his needs are important. When she behaves as the helper God made her to be, her husband experiences a fulfillment that could only be designed by God.

He is the source from which God gave her life. She realizes great joy and fulfillment as she steps to his side, takes his hand, and embraces her role as God's greatest gift. The fight for dominion is over. She chooses to serve because she reflects the character of God. The curse is undone because the Holy Spirit enables her to love as Christ loves, to serve unselfishly. It isn't demeaning. It is the generous heart of God flowing out in her behavior.

Husbands Must Submit—Unconditionally

I realize men reading this chapter are quite thrilled at this point. Hold on, Paul deals with you as well. In fact, Paul spends twice as much space on instructions to men than he does on wives. While there is much debate in homes across the world about the implications of this fact, we must at least admit Paul felt that men need some pretty serious instruction.

Paul begins his instruction to the men in Ephesians 5:28. Remember, however, this is nothing more than an explanation of how a man is to live out the command to submit to his wife—yes, *submit*. He is to *agape* his wife. Agape is the unconditional love that reflects the holy character of God. It is absolute generosity, absolute sacrifice, always aimed at the good of the other person. Our needs have nothing to do with the decision to give. In fact, we are to love unconditionally, regardless of the amount of love we receive in return.

This isn't sexual love. While that is an amazing gift of God between a man and wife, the command here is to love without expectation of anything in return. This isn't rubbing her back twenty minutes before bed, hoping to warm her up to your romantic side. This is, "I will die for you if I need to. I am going to give you everything you need, and I don't expect anything back.

Paul gives a context to the love. He is to love her as his own body. Paul reminds us God brought this wonderful gift from our own bodies. God knew exactly what man needed for fulfillment. She is God's perfect answer to man's deepest need. Out of reverence for God's design and His sacrifice on the cross, men are to treat this gift of God with the same generous lavishing of love Christ poured out on man.

It doesn't matter if she deserves it or not. I am not obligated to her, but to God. It doesn't matter if time draws a million wrinkles across her smile. It doesn't matter if life is good, bad, or in between. It doesn't matter if we have a lot or a little. It doesn't matter if she meets my expectations or disappoints me. I have been given this one command—love her unconditionally. She is God's gift. This is how I submit myself in reverence to Christ.

Recapture the WOW

In the middle of studying for this material, I had one of those awe-filled moments. My wife was playing some game on her laptop. I sat down on the ottoman in front of the couch and interrupted her game and said her name. "Diana."

She glanced at me and then back to her game. "I'm busy."

"Diana, look at me."

She was getting a little perturbed now. "What?" She locked eyes with me, and I smiled.

"You are the best gift God has ever given me!" She looked at me like I had lost my mind. I was honestly giddy inside. It didn't do much for her at that moment, but I was learning to stop and embrace the joy of the gift. It is amazing how passion rebounds when a man takes the time to look at his wife with a sense of gratitude to God for her place in his life.

I'm not saying guys should turn into blubbering packages of overflowing sappiness. However, it is important that we not focus on what is imperfect with our wives and relish in the beautiful reality that God has poured into them the things He knows we need to experience true intimacy.

I believe when we start worshipping God in thanksgiving for the gift wives are, something changes in our hearts that makes us more capable of showing unconditional love. It comes from our hearts, and we experience the kind of lavishing love God poured out on us in Christ.

One Word Wrap-up: Submit

Paul finishes his instructions by reminding us that each partner expresses submission in unique ways. "However, each one of you also must love his wife as he loves himself, and the wife must respect her husband" (Ephesians 5:32).

Husband, you must walk away from dominance and oppression. You are to submit by unconditionally giving of yourself so that your love is lavished to the same extent Christ's love was lavished on you. Then you will be able to walk away from the effect of the curse. You must not lord over her, but love her sacrificially—even if you never receive a thing in return.

Wife, you must regain the sense of awe that comes from the realization that God brought your life through man's side. The man you stand beside may not be perfect, but he is God's gift to you. You have a God-ordained responsibility to love him, walk next to him, and help God meet his needs.

If one's thinking is dominated by the need to be treated fairly, none of this will work. Spouses will never meet each other's expectations. They will always fall short of God's glory. However, if the Holy Spirit dominates our thinking, we can exude the generous heart of God. We can love when it isn't deserved. We can give when the gift isn't returned. We can continue to love, even when we are being treated unkindly. We can find the energy to pour ourselves out, even when we are exhausted. We can choose to not quit just because we are going through an ugly phase of our relationship. We can find joy in putting their needs ahead of our own. And when others say life isn't fair, we will look at the cross of Christ, refuse to count our sacrifice as worthy of repayment, and choose to serve out of reverence for what He did for us.

5

GENEROSITY IN MARRIAGE PART 2:
BEING A HELPMATE

∾

Let's Get Practical

In the last chapter we looked at the biblical call to restore the partnership of Eden. We are to embrace God's intended role for us as helpmates. This is the reflection of the character of God—His goodness, His generosity. In this chapter we are going to get very practical on a few of the more common issues many couples face as they try to live out the generosity of God in the reality of marriage. While the list of issues is not exhaustive, it is my hope that this will encourage you to begin asking God to help you express His generous spirit through your decision to serve your spouse as Christ serves you.

Give When You Aren't Receiving

There are periods in marriage when one of the spouses feels he or she is the only one giving. Regardless of whether or not that is an accurate perception, it takes grace to keep serving when one feels there is no reciprocation.

Nobody Cares

There may be times when one spouse feels emotionally dead. If either spouse has reached that point and is dependent on the other to express affection, adoration, appreciation, or a host of other emotions in order to keep giving, he or she will give up.

Generosity in marriage is a reflection of Christ on the cross. Sometimes it feels as if we are being crucified and nobody is paying attention or cares about the pain or frustration we are experiencing. In those moments we can turn to God and ask for divine mercy to keep giving. It is our only hope.

It comes down to a question of whether or not we intend to give as an act of worship or stubbornly insist that our family honor us for our gift. This is the moment when the difficult decision to walk away from a back-scratcher mentality can transform our ability to love our family as Christ loved us.

Giving from God's Heart

Brent and Lynn love the Lord with all their hearts, but life has a way of stripping away any sense of security. Lynn's emotional illness burst on and off the scene of their marriage with unannounced brutality. There was little warning to help them prepare for the episodes. One day Lynn was just fine, and the next the illness took over and her ability to cope with life was gone. It was frightening for both of them, and they found too few answers as they sought God's plan. Their life together was in a state of chaos.

Lynn's bipolar issues were debilitating for her and overwhelming for Brent as he became a single parent and took on running the household when Lynn was incapacitated. He was dealing with the sense of anger with God and frustration over his inability to help his wife. Lynn was trapped in a life of extreme highs and extreme lows. After a while, Brent's exhaustion was more than he could take; he never knew when the storm would hit again.

There was a period of a year and a half when things seemed better; the episodes were less frequent and less prolonged. Fall had always been particularly hard for Lynn, but this year when the trees turned and the snow blew, Lynn remained stable. Their hopes were high—maybe God had healed her! Could it be the period of desperation was over?

It was spring when the signs began to reappear. Brent was immediately desperate. *I can't do this! Lord, You promised to heal us when we pray!* The exhausting routine took over again: trips to the doctor, adjustments to the medication, bouts of crying and screaming. Would this nightmare ever end?

Lynn began coming out of the darkness again, but Brent felt emotionally dead with nothing left to give. He was angry at God and tired of being the one who had to hold it all together. He was out of resources and being very honest with God. *God, I don't know how to keep giving myself to her. I'm empty. How do I keep loving when I don't feel anything anymore?*

God surprised him by telling Brent that He wanted him to write down everything he loved about Lynn. *What?* Apparently God hadn't heard what Brent had just confessed. He didn't feel anything anymore; he didn't want to do this!

But the Holy Spirit wouldn't let up: *This is as much for you as it is for Lynn. When Satan throws the lies at you that cause you to question the strength of your love, I want you to be able to call out his lies.*

It was after dinner, a time Lynn was used to Brent poking around on the computer, so she didn't give it much thought when he spent the evening with the laptop. Little did she know that God was healing Brent's wounded heart through an exercise in generosity. God was forcing Brent to look beyond what was deserved and to see his wife through the Father's eyes. The "love list" God had required of him came slowly at first. But the more Brent wrote, and the more he refocused his heart on what was right about his wife, the more the Holy Spirit brought hope and joy and love to his barren heart.

Brent took his list to Lynn. "I really felt the Holy Spirit telling me to take some time and create this list for you. I want you to know I love you. Here are just a few of the reasons why."

The list was seventy-two items long! As Lynn read, God restored her soul. It was a pivotal moment in which she learned what it meant to be loved unconditionally. "It brought a sense of stability back to my heart. He was very specific. The things he said weren't vague. I mean he was really specific!"

Brent reflects on that difficult challenge as the point at which life began to change for both he and Lynn. "That's when things began to change. She gained the confidence that I wasn't going to leave her—that my love for her was real and deep."

Today, Brent and Lynn are more in love than ever. It started with an exercise in generosity.

Brent's response wasn't a matter of personal fortitude. He readily admits, "I didn't want to write that list." God made him. God was teaching him about the power of letting go of his fairness scale and just choosing to love with the unconditional passion of the Father. It changes hearts and brings hope where darkness seemed impenetrable.

When we listen to the generous heart of the Father and choose to lavish love on our spouse, especially during times when they simply cannot reciprocate, we are entering into the miraculous territory of transformational love! There are no limits to the ways that kind of generosity can bring healing and health to what was dead. Yes, there are moments when we look to heaven and honestly admit, *I have nothing left to give. I can't go on.* That is honest and real.

But God has the ability in those moments to empower our hearts to give just one more time. It flows out of some resource that isn't natural to our broken hearts. As God gives grace, and we lavish love, resurrection comes! That is the hope of a generous life—to give as God gave, because we believe nothing is so dead that it cannot rise again.

Create Sabbath for Your Spouse

One cannot give to his or her spouse when feeling emotionally depleted and has nothing left to give. When Jesus was tired He got alone to pray and refresh His Spirit. He reminded us that God gave us the Sabbath for our own good. That rest doesn't have to take place on a Sunday, but we must learn that when life is exhausting we have to find time to replenish the soul. This is especially true when one is feeling completely empty of emotion. We need to be filled so that we can be poured out.

Early in our marriage I didn't understand that people are reenergized differently. I knew what I needed, but I was clueless as to what my wife needed to feel regenerated.

I am an extreme extrovert, while my wife is an introvert. She gains energy and strength from time alone; I draw energy from time spent with other people. When I was a youth pastor, I spent my days alone in my office at the church or maybe occasionally with one or two teenagers. She spent her days in the middle of a great deal of commotion in her cubicle surrounded by dozens of other cubicles. By the end of the day we were both exhausted and needed to relax and refresh. Because neither of us understood how the other accomplished that, most days ended with the same unsettling exchange.

I would walk in the door and demand, "Come on. We're going to the mall. I've got to get out of here."

Diana cringed. "There is no way I'm going anywhere. I just got home! And I definitely don't want to go to the mall!" In my immaturity, I thought she just didn't care about my needs.

Sometimes the difficulties we face in giving to each other are simply misunderstandings about how our spouse is wired. Years later, when I realized what was going on, I tried an experiment. I knew Diana needed to refuel as much as I did, and I wanted to find a way to meet her need. I also knew I needed to meet my own need to reenergize. I thought I couldn't help her until I took care of myself. The Lord provided the insight and spirit to put her needs first.

Diana and I got home about the same time, and I could tell she was worn out from the day. "Diana, I'll make you a deal." The skepticism showed on her face. "I need to have some people time, but I know that does not appeal to you right now. So how about you go upstairs and enjoy a long bath while I cook dinner? You take thirty or forty-five minutes just for yourself. Then we can enjoy dinner together. After dinner, if we could just go walk around the mall for a while, it would really help me relax too. What do you think?"

Her jaw dropped open. "Who are you? What have you done with my husband?"

I was surprised by her response and by how good it made me feel. It was one of the first times I realized there is great fulfillment in focusing on your spouse's needs rather than demanding your own needs be met. Generosity is about relationship. It flows out of my respect for God and blossoms when it becomes about meeting the needs of the person God has given to me.

You can give only from what God gives you, and you can receive from God only when you stop to refresh your Spirit. Sometimes that takes place at church, and other times it doesn't. Either way, we give to others from what flows through us.

Be Patient During the Ugly Phases

"For better for worse, for richer for poorer, in sickness and in health." Most couples are too naive to know what all that commitment entails. Marriage is one of those things that grows richer with life, especially when life is rough. There are going to be phases that are uncomfortable. There are also phases that could be called just plain ugly. The secret for keeping a generous spirit during the ugly times is to embrace your spouse as your God-given partner rather than as the problem.

Remember: It's Just a Season

In the early years of marriage—and sometimes even after a couple has been together for a long time—the problem period seems as if it is never going to end. Each argument feels like the end of the world, and it is crushing to go through periods that are so difficult the romance is squeezed out by the pressures. During these times it is tempting to demand that one's own needs be met *first*.

I've pastored enough years to have watched couple after couple go through this. When a huge pressure or crisis hits the family and the stress mounts, previously tolerated flaws that each spouse has endured in the other suddenly becomes intolerable. Intimacy is replaced with irritability, and romance is replaced with disgust and discord. It feels as if the marriage is breaking up. It's moments like this couples must look to heaven and say to God, *For better or worse, right?*

When you feel that you're living in a "for worse" moment, remember: it's only a phase. A generous spirit holds its tongue, knowing that tomorrow isn't going to be as bad as today. Give grace to the one you love, and protect the gift God gave you.

On Different Pages Spiritually?

When one spouse is growing spiritually and the other isn't living up to his or her spiritual potential, it can be difficult to be the one who keeps giving. One of the couples we pastored told me an amazing story of spiritual awakening.

The wife and children had begun coming to church and had really gotten straight with God. It was an exciting time for them as their relationship with God began to blossom and they were finding spiritually fulfilling relationships in the faith community. The husband could see the new emotions and excitement in his wife but was obviously observing from a distance.

His wife kept encouraging him to come to church, and she and her friends prayed for him and believed God would touch him. The husband remained unconvinced.

Sometimes generosity resembles spiritual warfare. It's pointless to try to browbeat a spouse into a relationship with God. Faith must be lived out in an undemanding, serving posture to the unbelieving spouse. The Holy Spirit uses the generous patience and faith of the believing spouse to transform the unbelieving spouse.

In the end, this particular husband came to Christ. He later told me, "I was concerned that she had gotten wrapped up in some kind of cult. I held back in case I needed to get her out." Ironically, he was actually showing a generous spirit toward his wife.

God is able to use one spouse's generosity to reach a spouse who isn't where he or she should be spiritually. Remember Paul's command to reach an unbelieving spouse with a gentle spirit, not demanding conformity or issuing threats.

Those who oppose him he must gently instruct, in the hope that God will grant them repentance leading them to a knowledge of the truth, and that they will come to their senses and escape from the trap of the devil, who has taken them captive to do his will. —2 Timothy 2:25-26

Generosity is a reflection of God's character. As Christ is lifted up in one's actions, the spouse is drawn to Him.

Don't Give Up When They Blow It

When one spouse has embraced his or her God-called role to walk at his or her spouse's side, there is a holy patience displayed that God uses to transform the hurting marriage.

Fred Kelly was a good churchman. His guitar was his ministry. When he and his family sang, people experienced God. His spirit was rich, and his love for his wife, Phyllis, was undeniable.

Fred carried a small Bible, and it was part of his preparation for his music ministry. He made notes next to scriptures and marked down songs that fit the message of the scripture. He saw God's Word as part of the music and music as flowing from God's Word.

Phyllis loved Fred deeply, and Fred wanted to provide everything he could for Phyllis. He often sacrificed to bring her gifts. Sometimes he went a little overboard and stretched his generosity in ways he couldn't really afford. His motive was good—he loved Phyllis and wanted to give her the best. However, sometimes his plans backfired.

That was never truer than when he enacted his plan to build Phyllis her dream home. He couldn't afford the perfect house right away, so he reasoned he would build a house and sell it for a profit, build another and sell it for a profit, and so on. Before long, he figured, he would have enough money to build Phyllis her dream house.

However, the economic conditions in the country worsened. Fred had invested too much into the new house, and he couldn't afford to keep it for long. However, the housing market fell apart, and he was stuck. It wasn't long before the potential for losing the house was real. The pressure was crushing.

Fred's brother lived in California and played around with prospecting for gold. Gold prices were skyrocketing, and the allure of prospecting on the West Coast held a romance in Fred's heart. He was feeling like a failure in Illinois, and his house was a daily reminder that he wasn't taking care of Phyllis. He wanted to be more, and the thought of starting over in California was tempting.

There are moments in our lives when we are so concerned for our own wellbeing that our selfishness distorts our ability to see how our actions are hurting those around us. Fred was about to go through one of those times.

The more he thought about California, the more he became convinced he needed to leave his family in Illinois and head for a better life in California. One morning, that is exactly what he did. His self-absorbed demand for a "fair shake" left his church shocked and his family humiliated and angry.

Fred was double-minded. He wanted his own life, but felt guilty for leaving his family. Over the next months he would come home for a while then disappear again to his new life.

Phyllis was humiliated and hurt. The man who was her partner was treating her with total disregard. The kids coped as best they could, but this behavior didn't fit with their memory of a dad who loved the Lord and loved his family. The nightmare continued for some time.

Fred called home one night to tell Phyllis he didn't think he loved her anymore. He had chosen a path that included no one but himself, and he was ready to leave the person God placed at his side.

The people at church were understandably angry that he had chosen such horrific behavior. They encouraged Phyllis to let him go. He didn't deserve her, they said. She was justified to leave him and rebuild a life with someone who would love her and honor their commitment to each other.

Phyllis' response is one of the most amazing examples of a woman who embraced the generous grace of God toward her helpmate. She refused to buy into the advice of friends that marriage is only worth fighting for when both people are fighting. If she had to fight for her marriage by herself, then she would pray and fast and bring the Holy Spirit to bear on her hurting husband.

That is exactly what she did. Every single night this brokenhearted lady poured herself out before God for her husband's restoration. She wasn't just going to fuss at God for the unfair circumstances in which she was living; she was going to call out to God for the miracle nobody else believed could happen. She was going to believe in a future for Fred and with Fred, a future Fred had abandoned.

Week after week, month after month, Phyllis prayed and fasted and wept before God. Everyone else had given Fred over to a life of sin. However, it just wasn't in Phyllis to abandon her husband, even though he had abandoned her.

Something happens in us when we receive that kind of sacrificial love. The Holy Spirit can use the servanthood of a faithful spouse to reach the depths of a partner's soul in ways that arguing and guilt cannot.

Phyllis ran across Fred's little black worship Bible and began looking through it. She found a note alongside a passage in Romans. Fred had written in the margins "the broken vessel." Under these three words he scribbled the title of a song— "Because He Lives." The song talks about finding hope in the middle of painful periods of life. Our hope is found in the one final reality—Christ lives and, because He lives, our lives are worth living.

Phyllis found the unbelievable mercy she needed to lavish love on her husband. She began writing words of encouragement and faith in Fred's Bible. Next to "Because He Lives" Phyllis wrote a note to her husband. "Fred, Honey, I love you, and I'm praying for you day and night. Love always, Your Bible Wife, Phyllis."

She underlined "Day and Night" and "Bible" several times. She wasn't kidding. Everything in her was sacrificing her needs in order to meet his. Her commitment had nothing to do with his worthiness to receive such love. She was treating him in this way because her relationship to God would not allow her to do anything less. She wrapped up the Bible and mailed it to her prodigal husband.

Phyllis's faithfulness finally broke through the stubborn selfishness in Fred's heart. The Holy Spirit used Phyllis's consistent servanthood over those couple years to restore Fred. Phyllis went to California in a crowning moment of not giving up, and she came home with Fred.

The days ahead were not easy as Fred and Phyllis worked through the process of forgiveness and reconciliation. However, it's important to note that when God restores a relationship through generous love, He doesn't intend to bring them back half-way. He intends to bring abundant life to those who repent. And that is what He did for Fred and Phyllis.

A few years later Fred was lying in bed; cancer had left him only a few days to live, and he talked about that difficult period with a sense of gratitude. Fred and Phyllis's daughter, Cindy, was amazed at her father's words: "It was better the second time around."

Fred wasn't justifying the pain he had caused his family or claiming that it was in any way good for him to have gone through such a horrific mid-life crisis. But he had realized something about the love that flows between a husband and wife who have found a way to embrace their helpmate roles. Those things that could destroy us become the very things God uses to remind us that we are unconditionally loved. When we lock eyes with a husband or wife who has proven he or she won't abandon us, even when there is nothing to be gained in return, our love is transformed. We leave the fickle love of youth and learn the sacrificial and transformational love of Christ: agape love.

When a back-scratching demand for fair treatment controls one's mind it is difficult to comprehend the beauty and love that comes from sacrificial serving. We look at someone like Phyllis and rebel against her faithfulness for fear that God might ask us to do the same.

I am not saying that every marriage can be saved. Each partner has to choose to follow God's call in order to find marital healing. But I am saying that we can pray for the power to keep our own behavior in line with Christ's model of generous love. When we do that, God is able to transform hearts and bring healing.

In our own strength we can't live out that kind of love, but when the Holy Spirit enables us to love as Christ loves, hope for restoration becomes our indescribable peace. It allows us to keep giving when our barrel is empty, to keep hoping when there is no life left in the relationship, and to keep fighting for reconciliation when everyone else is advising us to admit it is over.

My prayer for you is that God will enable you to love as Christ loves us. He doesn't give up when we blow it. He believes in our tomorrow when everyone else has pronounced our death sentence. Even as Christ was nailed to a cross, He prayed for the salvation of His crucifiers. It is His model that should define how we apply generosity to our relationships. It is His unending belief that we will be more tomorrow than we are today that gives us the ability to not give up.

Put the Needs of Others First and Everybody Wins

Generosity is often expressed in relationships as finding out what the other person needs and then doing everything possible to make it happen. Putting your spouse's needs ahead of your own is part of what Paul taught in Ephesians as an act of generosity. In fact, when Paul calls us to use speech that is "useful," he uses the same word Jesus uses to define His own character as good and generous. Listen to Paul's instruction

> Let no evil talk come out of your mouths, but only what is useful for building up, as there is need, so that your words may give grace to those who hear. —Ephesians 4:29

In other words, when you talk to your spouse, use language that meets his or her needs. When you do that, God delivers His grace. Gary Chapman, in his book. *The Five Languages of Love.* (Chapman, 1992) defines five ways we communicate love. Each person has a preferred love language. When we receive expressions of love through that love language we more naturally understand the love being expressed to us.

Many times we fail to meet our spouse's needs because we are speaking a language he or she doesn't understand. The five languages of love set out in Chapman's book are words of *affirmation, physical touch, quality time, acts of service,* and *receiving gifts.* It is important to understand that a generous spirit chooses to express love in the way our spouse needs to receive it rather than the ways we want to receive it.

When we choose to be generous we quit asking *When are my needs going to be met?* and focus on communicating to our spouse in a way that meets his or her needs. William F. Harley Jr. gives us an even deeper understanding of a spouse's needs in his book, *His Needs Her Needs.* (William F. Harley, 2001) He explores the primary emotional needs of men and women and gives us very practical handles on living out the generous spirit to which Paul refers.

What Does He Need?

Sexual Fulfillment: Generosity in marriage means paying close attention to your husband's libido. In 1 Corinthians 7:5, Paul instructed us to be careful in this regard.

Recreational Companionship: Boys never really grow up, so don't neglect having fun. If you let someone else take up his playtime, you are giving away intimacy God designed for the two of you to share.

An Attractive Spouse: Be generous to your husband by maintaining your outward appearance. Freshen up for him as much as you did when you were dating.

Domestic Support: Do your part to keep your home a peaceful place he wants to be.

Admiration: Be proud of him. Be his number-one fan.

What Does She Need?

Affection with No Strings Attached: Give her affection without the expectation of sex in return.

Conversation: Talk to her. Stop and listen. And not just during halftime.

Honesty: Be truthful. Don't hide purchases or try to protect her by withholding information.

Financial Support: She doesn't need to be rich, but she needs you to take care of the family and provide a sense of stability.

Family Commitment: Be a good husband and father. When you show love to your children, you show your love for her.

It is important to understand that acting with generosity is a conscious choice to respect our partner's emotional needs. When we choose to meet his or her need without demanding anything in return, everyone's needs are met without the use of shame or blame. Love is freely given out of a desire to meet our partner's deepest needs. Intimacy and love are the result.

This is the very opposite of the kind of back-scratching relationships we have been taught to embrace. I have heard many couples admit to something like, "Our marriage is a 50/50 proposition." Contracts may be 50/50, but marriages are not. Marriage must be a generous display of God's love as we seek to meet the emotional needs of our spouse. When God gave us a spouse, He expected us to give as Jesus gave—to lay down our lives as a living sacrifice. That is holy and pleasing to God.

That principle is difficult to follow under one's own power. It requires a steady flow of the Holy Spirit in order to keep giving as Christ gave. That comes through prayer, knowledge of scripture, and fellowship with other Christians. Giving with this kind of depth isn't easy, and it doesn't come naturally. As God flows through us, our generosity reflects the unrestricted love of Christ.

End the Competition: Collaborate

When sin infected the character of Adam and Eve, one of the fundamental changes that occurred in their relationship was the end of partnership and the beginning of competition. They started fighting to see who would be the boss, and it hasn't ended to this day. The mind controlled by our sinful selves wants its own way, and that means we fight against what our spouse needs. That must change if we are to experience a restoration of the generous spirit of God in our marriages.

Diana and I married at the end of our junior year in college. Looking back, we realize we were very young and immature, selfish, and bullheaded. Most young couples experience turmoil early-on in their marriages, and we were no different.

After pushing each other's button for a few years, we were exhausted from the ongoing fight for control.

I was walking through the bookstore at Moody Bible Institute on a solo trip to Indiana. We owned a home in Fort Wayne that needed painting, and Diana was in South Dakota working. This half-day stop in Chicago to visit my brother led me to a bookstore where my attention was captured by the title of a book: *The Fight Free Marriage* (Anastasi, 1995). I remember thinking that a fight-free marriage seemed like an impossible achievement. But if there was any hope of such a thing, I wanted to know about it. I bought the book and spent the next two weeks painting during the day and reading at night. It changed my marriage.

Anastasi's primary point is that we must learn to quit competing to win a victory over our spouse and start collaborating to find solutions that meet both our needs. I found a few of his insights very helpful.

It is important to recognize that most of our conflicts are nothing more or less than a difference in personality. Once we learn why our spouse behaves as he or she does, we are able to communicate and collaborate in a way that helps us work together to find a solution.

Most fights are simply the result of impatience. We know what we want and we fight for it. If we can embrace a generous approach to marriage that begins with a radical commitment to understand and meet our spouse's needs, we are free to take the time necessary to find solutions that meet their needs. When both spouses are working at that, it takes more time, but the needs of both spouses are met.

We are also creatures of habit. We take selfish patterns of conflict resolution, aimed at getting what we want, into married life. We need to back up and relearn how to deal with our spouse's needs. Instead of pushing his or her buttons, we need to meet his or her need.

If we begin with an understanding of who our spouse is and how he or she thinks, we can build a decision making process that helps rather than conquers our spouse. Unless the Holy Spirit transforms our hearts into helpmates, we will tend to focus on gaining dominion rather than resolution.

Finally, we can commit to collaboration rather than competition. Collaboration means that we are committed to finding a solution in which neither spouse has to give up his or her needs. It requires an investment of time and a willingness to meet the spouse's needs. We can come to work as partners when we realize our spouse is not the problem; the problem is the problem. And as partners, spouses can work together to find a resolution to the problem.

Work Toward the Ideal Until You Embrace It

Most of us struggle with selfishness. We don't naturally think about what is best for anyone other than ourselves. However, with the Holy Spirit's help we can learn to live as a helpmate rather than a competitor. Many times that means moving toward the ideal goes more slowly than we would like. It also means investing at least as much energy into our spouse as we do into our own agenda.

Many couples think of marriage as two individuals on two individual journeys. I've heard many couples say things such as,

"We just grew apart, that's all." But marriage is to be two individuals on a *single* journey. It starts becoming "my journey" when I don't stop holding my spouse close to me with each step. If I quit paying attention to my spouse's needs we end up on separate trails.

My wife and I took a group of teenagers on a Tennessee wilderness adventure. We spent several days hiking through state forests. It was an amazing experience. However, by the end of the last day, everyone was exhausted and it was difficult to stay positive. Complaints and tempers were on the rise.

Our guides stopped us for some instruction. "We only have one mile left before the completion the journey. But, there's a problem. The rest of the trail is a steep incline, and it is going to be more than tough. It is going to take every ounce of energy you have left—and then some. If you don't work together, some of the team won't make it. So here is what we are going to do.

"We are going to stay within one step of each other. You will look to the person ahead of you. That person will be a foot or two higher than you with each step. It's that steep. You will have to reach a hand upward and let the other person grip your arm. You will have to put your entire strength into making each step. You will make it because the other person helps you.

"After you have taken your step, you will need to get a strong foothold and turn around to lift up the person behind you. You will reach behind you, get a solid grip on that person's arm, and when you both are ready, pull.

"It will feel as if you are the only one working at it. I assure you the person is giving it all they've got. Don't yell or complain for that person to try harder. Instead, be encouraging and let the other person know you will not let go or give up. You both will hurt. But, you both will make it to the top if you just keep reaching up and then reaching down."

It is an amazing picture of generosity in marriage. To give as Jesus gave means we are going to have to reach above us for support and help. We don't have the energy we need to make it through this journey. God is going to have to give us strength to take the difficult steps we need to take in order to grow. Once we have received the help we need from above, we can use our position to reach back and help our spouse.

We can't afford to take two steps by ourselves. If we do, we will get separated from our spouse. Their needs have to be just as important as our needs. We grow so that we can help meet their need. We can't do that without God's intervention. But, when we focus on growing closer to God and then provide the strength and help our spouse needs, we are assured we will complete the journey together.

When our youth group reached the top of that one mile incline, we all collapsed. Something had changed, though. Our complaining and fighting had ended. The encouragement of our teammates had really helped us all make it. We found transformation in those difficult moments. We knew what it was to need and give. The generous spirit our team members displayed became our own generosity as we helped those behind us. We had all lived the same struggle and had worked together to find the strength to prevail.

That is the effect of generosity on marriage. Where others are destroyed by the difficult realities of life, we draw close to each other. We choose to give out of the grace given to us. We refuse to blame and cast shame. We reach the top just as exhausted as others, but end up far closer to one another than those couples who fight their way up the hill.

As we wrap this up, it is important to be very honest with each other. Staying generous toward our spouse is difficult. You won't do it perfectly. However, if you focus on the amazing gift God has given you, and accept your obligation to God to care for that precious gift, you can serve without feeling abused or used. You can give when others would quit. You can express the character of God who delivered a generous portion of love and grace even though we didn't deserve it.

When we do that we understand that Jesus wasn't calling us to be wimps who simply allow others to walk all over us. We don't turn the other cheek and walk the extra mile because we are wimps. We do that because we have chosen to embrace the generous heart of God who gives more than is deserved so that we can become more than we are today. In marriage we embrace this godly character so that we can experience the full blessing offered us in the gift of our spouse.

6
GENEROSITY IN PARENTING

No Pat Answers

As we begin this discussion on generosity in parenting, I must admit I feel completely inadequate on the subject; I believe most parents do. Applying the principles of generous living to parenting can seem confusing. On one hand, we understand we don't treat children as they deserve to be treated. On the other hand, we must embrace the call to discipline our children. Both are biblical.

So how do we apply the principle of going the extra mile and turning the other cheek to raising children? Our prayer is that we won't spoil them or crush them. It's a predicament that haunts all parents who care about their children's spiritual wellbeing.

I want to be very careful, and I don't want you to think there is an easy fix for parents who are trying to figure this out. Every child is a little different and all require different mixtures of grace and discipline.

My two sons are as different as night and day. My oldest responds quickly. His heart is soft and it doesn't take much to bring him back into line. In fact, sometimes I have to encourage him to stand up for his opinion when it is different than mine.

My youngest son, on the other hand, is quite stubborn and enjoys the challenge of debating his parents. The other day he was pushing my buttons and I was doing my best to maintain my cool. *Be generous, Kevin! Be generous!* I muttered under my breath.

He heard me. "Yeah, Dad. Be generous. Just do what I want."

That about did it for me. "Son, I'm not going to kill you right now. That is generosity in this moment!"

A few days later he and I were walking into the entrance of Wal-Mart. He started in again. "You know, Dad, I've decided you're right. I'm going to be generous and let you buy me something in here." He laughed.

Joking back, I said, "That's not fair!"

He quickly responded, "It's fair for me!"

We both laughed. At least he is getting it enough to make jokes about it.

Applying the proper amount of grace and discipline is a rough proposal. We pray and pray for help yet never quite feel as if we're getting it right. Paul gives us some help in Ephesians 6 as he continues to instruct us on how to submit to one another out of reverence for Christ.

Remember, the key principle of generosity is putting our own needs behind the needs of the other person. A generous person gives regardless of the other person's worthiness—loves regardless of the other person's loveliness. The generous person is gracious because of God's grace, not because of the other person's behavior.

Paul applies these concepts to the relationship between parents and children:

> Children, obey your parents in the Lord, for this is right. "Honor your father and mother"—this is the first commandment with a promise: "so that it may be well with you and you may live long on the earth." And, fathers, do not provoke your children to anger, but bring them up in the discipline and instruction of the Lord. — Ephesians 6:1-4 NRSV

Generosity as Obedience

Paul begins with the child and brings a simple principle to the forefront. "Want to live long? Do what your parents say!" I know to the adult this doesn't sound like too big a deal. However, to a teenager who believes his or her parents have lost their minds, this is a stretch.

It is important to help our children embrace a generous approach to their relationship with their parents. The fruitfulness of their lives hangs in the balance. So we must make sure we push the point.

Children should show generosity to Mom and Dad because they love God. Mom and Dad might be wrong; honor them anyway. As long as it isn't going to harm the child or anyone else, parents should be honored. Children should do what their parents tell them to do. God gave them parents to protect them and help them learn to follow God. They should make the choice to honor their parents because they love Jesus.

Awareness of Limits

This book, however, is for adults. So let's get into the difficult stuff. Paul gives us two applications to generosity in parenting—what we shouldn't do, and what we should do. Let's begin with his warning.

"Don't provoke your children to anger." Generosity in parenting begins with learning our children's emotional limits. We have the tendency to spend eighty percent of our parenting time as behavior police. We spend far too much time catching them in bad behavior and far too little time praising them for good behavior.

That can cause a great many problems. In their book, *How Full Is Your Bucket: Positive Strategies for Work and Life*, Tom Rath and Donald Clifton show that five uplifting comments can be undone by one careless word. The power of parents' words cannot be underestimated. Paul is calling us to amazing generosity.

Our children aren't grownups. That means they are going to blow it—probably more than we will. If we are going to keep them from falling into depression and anger, we are going to have to work at lifting up their strengths more than five times the amount we point out their shortcomings. If we focus on their weaknesses without pointing out their strengths at a far greater rate, we will crush them.

Each child has a different boiling point. It is our responsibility as parents to learn their emotional limits and always keep their needs at the forefront of our discipline techniques. The point of this book isn't to lay out discipline techniques, and we aren't going to spend any time there. I do want to make sure we understand that parenting with generosity means putting our children's needs first.

What We Should Do: Discipline Mixed with Instruction

Paul tells us we should bring children up in the discipline and instruction of the Lord. This two-pronged approach is important. Yes, we need to show mercy as we help them learn. But, a generous portion of mercy includes disciplining them for their own good.

They Need Grace

Stephanie and Steve Broomhead love the lord. They are committed Christians who were initiated into generosity as parents from the very beginning of Faith's life. She was premature, and those early days were difficult. The countless hours at the hospital, the mountain of medical bills, and the unending tiredness all confirmed that parenting this little girl was going to require a divine level of grace.

After miracle upon miracle, little Faith finally came home. It didn't take long before she had Steve wrapped around her little finger. She grew, began to walk, began to talk, and blossomed into a very lovely, stubborn, young lady.

Her beautiful eyes are matched only by her temper. It all depends on her mood. If she's in one of her moods, a butterfly surprising her on a walk might send her into a crying tantrum. Like many young children, she doesn't have the emotional maturity to handle difficult days without throwing a fit.

That can be tiring for young parents. But, Steve and Stephanie decided to institute the principle of grace in their home. So they began teaching Faith about grace in real life.

"Faith, you are misbehaving. You deserve to be punished, but Mommy and Daddy want you to understand what grace is. Grace is not giving you the punishment you deserve. That's what Jesus did for us. And even though you deserve to be punished, Mom and Dad are giving you grace."

Faith didn't receive grace every day. There were days when Stephanie and Steve let her know that she had gone too far and was going to be punished. That is the balance of the Father's mercy. Sometimes His mercy is to inflict enough pain that we don't want to misbehave anymore.

Faith must have been learning the lesson. She was having one of those "moody" days, and Stephanie's nerves were shot. Tantrum after tantrum ate away at Stephanie's willingness to withhold punishment. Faith must have known it. She had just let one of her emotional outbursts fly, and Stephanie's face turned red with anger. Faith realized she had pushed her mother one step too far. Faith's eyes got wide and she screamed, "Grace, Mommy! I need Grace!"

Steve and Stephanie's generosity in parenting is teaching Faith something about her relationship to God: she needs grace.

Teaching the Cost of Generosity

Instructing our children in generosity can be an exercise in the unexpected. My good friend Greg Clark is a pastor. He has five children who all love the lord and are serving

Him faithfully. One day when they were little, they came out of Sunday School all excited. They told Greg they were being challenged to raise money for missions. Each had received a cardboard quarter-saver with enough slots to hold twenty dollars in quarters.

Greg thought, *There is no way I can come up with a hundred dollars in quarters. These kids are going to learn a lesson about generosity.* He let his children know, if they were going to help the missionaries, they needed to sacrifice and find ways to raise the quarters from their own work. This was going to be their project, so Dad wasn't going to provide their quarters.

Cory was six at the time. He was the typical little guy with a mouth full of loose teeth. He listened and nodded, but really didn't catch the point that this was going to take work. Each of the other children spent the next several weeks doing all sorts of activities to earn the quarters to fill their cards.

The Sunday morning came when the children were to turn in their sacrificial offering. They piled in the car and headed for church. Cory sat in the seat directly behind Greg.

"Dad, do you have a quarter?"

"What do you need a quarter for, Cory?" Greg knew what was coming.

"I'm supposed to turn in my quarters for the missionaries, but I don't have any quarters."

It was time to teach Cory something about generosity—it takes work and sacrifice. "Cory, Daddy told you it was going to take sacrifice to earn money for missions. I can't just give you a quarter. You need to find a way to earn some money so that your gift is from your sacrifice."

"I know, Daddy. But, I really want to give something for missions."

It grew conspicuously quiet in the back seat. Greg assumed Cory was pondering his father's great wisdom. Then out of the silence, Greg heard a grunt.

"Ugggh!" Cory's little hand reached between the seats and offered his daddy one bloody tooth. He knew Greg was the tooth fairy, and Cory was willing to make the sacrifice! Greg gave him the quarter.

Cory is a twin. In his mind, he reasoned his brother, Chad, must also have a loose tooth. Cory leaned over to try to remove a tooth from his brother. After all, it was worth another quarter. Needless to say, Chad resisted. Apparently Chad decided the missionaries would need to pull their own teeth.

While I am not advocating our children remove body parts as an act of generosity, Cory's precious gift—as funny as it is—flowed from a heart that was learning the sacrifice of generosity.

We parents must understand that generosity is learned as we teach *and* discipline. One without the other is inadequate. Spare the rod, spoil the child. Overuse the rod, and the child's spirit breaks. It takes a deep dependence on the Holy Spirit for divine wisdom to know our children and to give them what they need when they need it.

Generous Love Transforms a Stubborn Heart

I was never very good at knowing when my children needed more grace or more discipline. I tend to be too much of a disciplinarian. I got it from my grandfather: yell first, ask questions later. I don't know how many times I've had to ask God to forgive my impatience. I've asked my children to forgive me quite a few times as well.

Daniel, my youngest, tends to push my buttons more than his brother does, so he and I have had some straightforward battles of the will. He is a teenager now, and I constantly pray for the wisdom to connect with him when difficulties arise. As God was teaching me to apply the principles of generosity, he used my son to open my heart to the amazing transformational power of undeserved mercy.

Daniel was outgrowing his room, so we decided to switch his bedroom and the boys' toy room. We had painted his new bedroom, and it was time for him to move the toys to the new toy room. He reluctantly headed upstairs to do the work.

Andrew was upstairs and knew just how grumpy Daniel was about the whole ordeal. Andrew was enjoying his brother's pain and was looking for an opportunity to get in a dig. Sure enough, Daniel reached for a pail of dominoes and it dropped. The dominoes went everywhere, and Andrew pounced on the opportunity. "Great job, Dan!"

Daniel blew his stack. He yelled at his brother, kicked him out of his new room, and screamed, "That's it. I'm not doing it. I'm done!" I knew his tantrum was intended for me. He was letting me know he was not happy, and he was challenging me to do something about it.

Normally, I would have walked upstairs gotten eye to eye with him, and quietly said something like "Go ahead. Make my day!" (Too many Clint Eastwood movies.) But, the Holy

Spirit grabbed my heart and wouldn't let me go. *Kevin! Trust me on this. Choose an act of generous love.*

I immediately fought back. *I can't let him get away with this, God. If I don't discipline him, how will he learn to not act like this?* I sensed God telling me to trust Him and reminding me of the times I had made a mess of things and had received grace.

That conversation with God took less than a minute, but I knew what I needed to do. I thought it was crazy and would lead to no good, but God wouldn't leave me alone. I was going to do something I didn't want to do.

I walked upstairs and headed into Daniel's room. He was expecting me and had postured himself to communicate his disgust. He was lying on his back with his arms folded behind his head. His face was hard with defensiveness. His jawline bulged as he clinched his teeth. He was ready for the fight.

I looked at him; he stared me down. I winked and walked passed him. I moved to his closet, got down on my knees, and without uttering a word started picking up the dominoes.

They were everywhere. I'm not sure how long it took to pick them up, but Daniel didn't utter a word. When they were all back in the pail, I stood up and turned around. Daniel's confusion peeked out from behind his stubborn stare. He looked at me, still defensive and angry, but obviously astonished at what was happening. It was if he was waiting for the lecture, but curiously unsure that it would come.

I smiled at him as I walked by. It wasn't a sarcastic smile. It was a smile that said, "It's okay. I understand you are frustrated. I'm going to help." It went against everything in me.

I knew this wouldn't work and was a horrible decision for a strong parent. But, God wouldn't let me do anything else.

I walked into the new toy room and put the pail on the shelf. When I walked back into Daniel's room I was astonished. He had completely relaxed. His face was no longer hard with anger.

Something was going on here, and I was learning as much, if not more, than Daniel. I sat down on his bed and started talking with him about his day tomorrow. He joined the conversation without hesitation. When we were through, I got up and said, "I love you, Dan."

"I love you too, Dad." He responded.

I went downstairs. My astonishment must have been visible on my face. My wife said, "What's wrong with you?" I told her what had just happened.

"I'm not saying that I should always ignore his temper; I think there is a time to inflict punishment. But, I am pretty sure God just gave me a wonderful picture of what can happen when grace is given in an undeserved measure. I watched that boy melt in ways my discipline has never produced."

I am not saying we shouldn't discipline our children. Two days later, I removed that same child's bedroom door because he slammed it.

I do believe we need to discipline children with punishment. But, I am learning that lavishing grace can be just as effective for transformation when applied at the Holy Spirit's prompting. There is something about applying the generous love of God that transforms a stubborn heart.

Generosity Isn't Enabling

There is a difference between offering undeserved grace at the moving of the Holy Spirit and enabling a child's poor behavior. It's important to be careful that our desire to protect our children doesn't cause us to shield them from the pain God will use to transform their hearts. I want to encourage you that godly discipline produces a harvest of righteousness. (Hebrews 12:11)

Finding Balance

You may be wondering how you will know when it's appropriate to discipline and when it's appropriate to show mercy. I wish I had that kind of wisdom. I don't. I only know that as parents trying to bring transformation into our children's hearts, we must stay close to the Spirit of God. We must pay close attention to His prompting. We won't always get it right. Others will often disagree with our parenting decisions. But, we need to do what God calls us to do, when He calls us to do it. The point is to stay focused on their transformation and not our revenge.

I've seen parents whose patience with a child seemed overboard. In some cases the result was destructive. Often, a child whose parents continually bailed him or her out of trouble seemed to never grow up. On the other hand, sometimes children with the same sort of upbringing find Christ and experience radical transformation. They testify to the amazing patience their parents displayed.

I've known other parents whose discipline appeared so unrelenting that I was sure their strict rules would end up running their children off. While some rebelled, others turned into wonderful Christian men and women. So which one is right and which one is wrong? What causes one child to find God and another to run away?

I think as parents we must realize that our children will make their own decisions about Christ. Sometimes they may blame their parents' lack of caring or heavy handedness for their choices. But, in the end, they make the choice.

As parents we must admit that we aren't God. We don't do this parenting thing perfectly. The promise of scripture keeps us full of hope: "Above all, maintain constant love for one another, for love covers a multitude of sins" (1 Peter 4:8 NRSV).

The principle of the extra mile is always upon the back of parents—don't give up on them. We give our children more than they deserve because we are choosing to instruct them in the generous love of God. Sometimes that love is expressed with discipline, and other times it is expressed as grace. At all times it flows from a heart that wants to lavish love so that our children can experience the transforming hand of God.

7
GENEROSITY IN RECONCILIATION

∽

We all have faced difficult or broken relationships. They can often be painful and ugly. To give someone who has hurt us better than they deserve is the last thing on our minds when we have been deeply wounded. It is during the times when we've been betrayed, disregarded as unimportant, or made to feel we don't matter that the idea of offering our offender the ability to hurt us again—to turn the other cheek—seems completely unfair.

Yet, if we are to seriously seek the character of God in our own hearts, we must come face to face with the reality that Jesus wants us to embrace a level of reconciliation that isn't limited by what is deserved. We must pick up our cross and follow Him into the painful journey of initiating reconciliation with those who don't deserve mercy.

It's Time to Eat

In New Testament days, to be invited to have dinner at someone's table was a special thing. It meant you were family, and it was taken very seriously. In fact, in *Dictionary of Jesus and the Gospels*, the authors informed that if one had a severe conflict with another and that person wanted to let the other know that he or she was no longer part of the family, the person might be kicked out and not allowed to eat at the offended person's table anymore. Imagine the scene. A father and son have such a strong argument that the son storms out of the house and the father bars the door and declares his son may no longer eat at his table. This is how a relationship was declared severed.

In our day, we might simplify it a little. We just quit calling him or her on the cell phone; no invitation is offered for popcorn and a movie, we quit writing, we let the person slip out of our life. We might even go so far as to snub him or her in public. If it is our spouse, we might sleep on the far edge of the bed and grunt in answer to a question. We might even refuse to offer affection or acknowledge his or her presence. We have plenty of ways to let someone know he or she is no longer embraced as family. But, in Jesus' day, one of the strongest demonstrations that a relationship was fractured was to not allow the person eat at the table.

When it was time to forgive, forgiveness was demonstrated by inviting the friend or family member back to the table. The act of inviting someone back was significant. It meant the person was restored as a family member.

This is the image Jesus had in mind when He makes the following statement in Revelations referring to His pattern for reconciliation. There are subtle differences from what we might expect in our culture today. Notice who initiates the reconciliation and what it implies about how we are to apply the principles of generosity to our broken relationships.

Those whom I love I rebuke and discipline. So be earnest, and repent. Here I am! I stand at the door and knock. If anyone hears my voice and opens the door, I will come in and eat with him, and he with me. (Revelation 3:30 NIV)

Jesus doesn't wait for an invitation to come eat at the table. *He* initiates the reconciliation before the person who kicked Him out of the family ever thinks of it. It doesn't matter that Jesus was the one rejected and hurt by the person who no longer wanted to be in the healthy relationship. His pattern is to take the first step.

The other amazing thing is that Jesus doesn't wait for the other person to show some form of interest before He starts letting it be known that He wants to heal the relationship. It isn't that He heard through the village rumor mill that His enemy wanted Him to make the first step. He goes to the house on His own volition, because that's the kind of God He is. He announces publicly that if one is willing to go through the effort necessary to remove the things that are keeping them apart, He will work through all that and bring healing to the relationship. It is this model of generosity in reconciliation that must become our pattern for healing broken relationships.

Beyond the Letter of the Law

This kind of generous reconciliation goes way beyond what the law requires. We live in a world that has unwritten rules about when it is appropriate to let down our guard enough to broach the subject of reconciliation. We learned the rules early: If the other person says "sorry" first, then we say we're sorry. Or we don't feel we did anything wrong so why should we have to apologize? Or, "She knows my number, she can call if she wants to talk to me." Or, "I have nothing to be sorry for, and I'm not going to make nice."

There are many more, but they all flow from the idea that reconciliation can only be expressed within the rules of fairness. If I am not treated fairly, there can be no reconciliation.

Jesus' behavior shows that the laws of fairness simply do not work in reconciliation. Reconciliation isn't based in rules of fairness but of grace. Reconciliation becomes possible only when someone cares more about healing the relationship than being repaid for the pain he or she has endured.

Initiating reconciliation does not mean we should ignore sin. What it means is that we begin with the acknowledgment that if we are going to wait until we are treated fairly before diving into the pain of healing a relationship, we may be destined to the loneliness of separation.

Like Jesus, we are called to take the posture of one who declares his or her commitment to initiate healing and then patiently waits at the door until the other party opens it.

Be the One to Go First

We have all had our feelings hurt and suffered the pain of being disregarded by someone we love. When that happens, the idea of being the one who has to initiate reconciliation seems like rubbing salt in an open wound. We ask ourselves, *Why should I have to put my heart on the line? Why am I the one who has to go first? Why must I be the one who has to patiently wait for him [or her] to open the door to our relationship?*

The reason is simple: that's what Jesus did for us. Before we ever began to think about renewing our relationship with Him, He knocked and then patiently waited, so he looks at us and reminds us, "a servant is not above his master" (Matthew 10:24). To reflect the generous grace of Jesus we must initiate reconciliation and wait for the one who has rejected our relationship to repent. We guarantee the one who has left us that we will not give up. We promise to do all that is within our power to heal the relationship. We *will* come in and sit down at the table.

When we take this posture we must be honest with ourselves. This is not a pain-free process. This kind of love leads to a cross, and it isn't easy or quick.

It may be that you knock on the door and wait and pray only to discover the other person is satisfied with things the way they are. They aren't going to open the door, and reconciliation never happens. They move on, they pass away, they don't acknowledge the separation. That can be a painful reality of knocking and waiting.

It is a road littered with emotional frustration. We are likely to encounter messes that will need to be cleaned up along the way. However, it is also a road that leads to a miraculous intervention of God where our love for each other is restored. It is the picture of Hosea, whose constant patience and ridiculous expressions of love reflect God's heart for the lost.

An Example of Hosea's Love

The book of Hosea gives us a picture of God's patience in reconciling with Israel. At God's command, Hosea marries an adulterous woman, Gomer. Her continued unfaithfulness causes Hosea great shame. Yet, God commands Hosea to keep going after her. God is using Hosea's persistence in reconciliation as a firsthand picture of God's unbridled love.

Therefore I am now going to allure her; I will lead her into the desert and speak tenderly to her. —Hosea 2:14

God intends to patiently wait as we come to the end of our selfish patterns. He allures us into those places where we realize that we are empty-handed. Nothing we thought was worthy of our love has proven itself as faithful as He has. And in the moments that we realize we are in danger, we see His faithfulness. His never-ending love wins us back to Him, and our relationship is restored.

This powerful picture of generosity in reconciliation is more than an ideal. It is God's pattern for how we should deal with the broken relationships in our lives. Joe Sanders displays a powerful examples of this godly patience.

Liz and Joe had been married for some time. They attended church together every week, but, they were suffering through some marital problems.

Liz had become infatuated with a coworker, and it was beginning to destroy their marriage. In the end, Liz walked away from the Lord and left her husband. Her unfaithfulness did not deter Joe's love though, and he began a long journey of showing a Hosea kind of love.

Most of us would have risen in anger and declared our biblical right to walk away from someone who didn't love us anymore. Joe refused to believe it was over, and he focused on loving Liz, even as she walked down the path of sin.

Joe, not known for romance, decided it was time to allure Liz into the desert. "I'm going to keep after her until she comes home. One of these days she will come to her senses, and I'll be here for her when she comes home."

For those who demand fairness, Joe's love makes no sense. But Joe was reflecting the heart of God, and God's love is unending. God refuses to allow us the naivety of believing we can maintain a relationship with Him while sinning against Him. However, He also keeps the door for reconciliation wide open as He continues to shower unbridled love on us. That is exactly what Joe was doing.

Joe wrote a love letter to Liz every day—he was standing at the door knocking. When her relationship with the co-worker fell apart, Joe was there to help her. He persistently and openly declared his desire to restore the relationship. When she moved into an apartment, Joe helped her move her things. He showed her what unconditional loved looked like. Day after day, Joe refused to walk out of her life. He patiently displayed a love that didn't make any sense.

Meanwhile, God was working on Liz's heart. She was waking up to the insanity of her actions. She would either continue down a road driven by emotion, or she would accept the unconditional love Joe had been showering on her. In the end, Liz came home.

Liz restored her relationship with God, accepted forgiveness from her husband, and experienced the power of generous love. If you ask Liz to talk about Joe as a husband, her eyes fill with tears. She tells of an unconditional love that changed her heart. You can see the tenderness of a woman who has been loved beyond what she deserved. Because of that kind of generosity in reconciliation, God has been able to restore Joe and Liz's love and heal the damage selfishness had wreaked upon their marriage.

They aren't living a fairy tale. Like every other couple, they have their struggles. But, God was able to use Joe's godly patience to bring true love back to their family.

Forgiveness and Trust

I have often talked with people just like Joe and Liz who are going through the broken relationships. Many times one or both of the parties involved have done something so hurtful that it is all but impossible for the offended one to forgive—let alone trust—the other person. Many times someone has asked "What if I don't trust him anymore?" or "What if I can't forgive her?" I have even heard some say things like, "I can forgive, but that doesn't mean I'm willing to spend time with him [her]."

These are honest expressions of our emotions. But, to embrace the heart of Jesus in our relationships we have to recognize that there is a difference between forgiveness, trust, and reconciliation.

Forgiveness is giving up the right to hold someone accountable to us for his or her sin. We transfer the judgment seat from ourselves to God. That is difficult. It takes an act of the Holy Spirit to cleanse one's heart of hanging on to the hurt. We feel we are owed something, that we have the right to revenge.

For restoration to happen, we must choose to ignore our rights. We are to look at the generous sacrifice of Christ and listen to His frank honesty about God's economy.

For if you forgive others their trespasses, your heavenly Father will also forgive you; but if you do not forgive others, neither will your Father forgive your trespasses. —Matthew 6:14-15 NRSV

Forgiveness is never deserved or earned, but we are required to offer it. It is always an act of grace. This is the most basic level of reflecting the generous character of God. In fact, forgiveness can be offered without any kind of repayment from the person being forgiven. Forgiveness originates in the heart of the forgiver. It means we forgive because forgiveness flows from our character, not from the other person's worthiness.

It feels dangerous to forgive because we open ourselves up to the possibility that we will be rejected again. Butch participates in a ministry to prison inmates that goes into prisons with one goal in mind: to introduce Jesus to the prisoners. They are not advocates for prisoners' rights or psychologists offering counseling. They are Christians introducing the love of Jesus to those who have offended.

This group of Christians devotes weekends to going into a prison and working through a series of Bible studies, discussions, and confessional activities with participating inmates. Each prisoner receives several dozen homemade cookies donated by church members.

It would be hard to overstate what this means to the prisoners. They rarely receive treats. One of the church members had included a box of strawberries, and one of the inmates ate one after another with obvious delight. Butch said to him, "You sure seem to be enjoying those. How long has it been since you've had a strawberry?"

"Twenty-four years," the man replied.

When the men receive the treats, they are given the following instructions. "These cookies are yours. You can do with them whatever you want. People who love you baked them. They don't want anything in return. You can eat them, save them, sell them, whatever you want. They are given with no strings attached. However, we want to encourage you to save the last dozen. At the end of this weekend you are going to be challenged to forgive someone in this prison. We are going to encourage you to take your last dozen cookies and give them to someone you need to forgive."

That might seem like a simple matter to those of us who don't live in prison. But that kind of peace offering can be understood as "weakness" in a system driven by position, power, revenge, and reciprocity.

Some of the men are in prison with people who have killed or raped their family members. Forgiveness in these circumstances is more than generous. It is a miracle. Yet time and time again these men find the grace of God necessary to go to people who don't deserve such mercy and offer them something as simple as a dozen cookies as a reflection of God's Spirit ruling their hearts. If men like this can offer forgiveness in such brutal circumstances, surely we can find the grace to offer forgiveness as well.

While forgiveness is offered freely, trust must be earned. Jesus wasn't naïve; He even instructed us: "See, I am sending you out like sheep into the midst of wolves; so be wise as serpents and innocent as doves" (Matthew 10:16 NRSV). If my child steals from me, I might forgive him quickly, but that doesn't mean I'm going to leave my wallet lying around. Jesus doesn't call us to be foolish.

If a spouse is abusive, Jesus doesn't ask us to blindly return to a setting where we are in danger. If a friend lies, Jesus isn't asking us to accept his or her word as gospel. We can forgive the person, but that doesn't mean we immediately trust the person. As the person turns away from the old ways and begins to make behavioral changes, we can begin to trust again as the trust is earned.

Beyond Trust and Forgiveness

Reconciliation moves beyond forgiveness and trust. It is the restoration of a healthy relationship. It cannot happen without forgiveness, and forgiveness cannot happen if one holds a grudge.

On the other hand, trust is developed in the middle of the process of coming back to a healthy relationship. One step after another, we begin the journey of knocking, declaring our intent to renew the relationship, opening ourselves to risk, and getting beyond those things that caused the separation in the first place. All the way along that journey we put our hearts on the line in small measures and experience a rebuilding of trust as each person proves his or her intent to love, and not harm, the other person. Trust is earned in the middle of the journey, not before reconciliation begins.

I can forgive someone without trusting the person. But there is no hope for full reconciliation without the restoration of trust. I can choose to trust yet refuse to reconcile. However, I cannot reflect the character of God without remaining willing to heal the relationship.

To go deeper, I cannot claim to have found reconciliation just because I tolerate the person. It might feel more comfortable to say, "Everything is right between us. I don't hold any ill will against John. I don't want to go to dinner with him, but I don't wish him harm." When the pretenses are stripped away, what that means is "I have offered forgiveness. But I am in no way willing to find true healing in our relationship." That is to offer forgiveness without following the pattern of reconciliation.

Reconciliation Demands Healing

Reconciliation is the healing of the relationship by removing the sins that have separated us. The liar has to quit lying in order for true reconciliation to be possible. The adulterer has to give up the cheating ways before the offended spouse can regain the trust necessary to find true healing.

Reconciliation is tough. It isn't as automatic and unencumbered as forgiveness. Neither is it as uninvolved as learning to trust someone. It takes time. Until someone decides to let down the guard and declare willingness to enter the messy and awkward journey of healing, neither party has hope of restoration.

Fractured Worship

Jesus knew reconciliation was important for us because true worship cannot happen when we have chosen to leave relationships fractured. Following is how Jesus explained the seriousness with which God views the issue.

> You have heard that it was said to those of ancient times, "You shall not murder"; and "whoever murders shall be liable to judgment." But I say to you that if you are angry with a brother or sister, you will be liable to judgment; and if you insult a brother or sister, you will be liable to the council; and if you say, "You fool," you will be liable to the hell of fire. So when you are offering your gift at the altar, if you remember that your brother or sister has something against you, leave your gift there before the altar and go; first be reconciled to your brother or sister, and then come and offer your gift. —Matthew 5:21-24

True reconciliation has to happen before we can worship. Our relationship with God, our ability to experience intimate worship, is ruined by relationships that are left undone. Our stubbornness and unwillingness to let go of our right to be asked for forgiveness destroys our relationship with God.

That is because true reconciliation flows from a character that reflects the holiness of God. This issue has to do with our commitment to live the life of love in the same way Christ loved us. He initiated our reconciliation. We are to imitate him. If we refuse to model this excessively generous approach to healing our relationships, we are rejecting his holiness.

Make every effort to live in peace with all men and to be holy; without holiness no one will see the Lord. See to it that no one misses the grace of God and that no bitter root grows up to cause trouble and defile many. —Hebrews 12:14

Living at peace is a reflection of the holy character of God. This is all associated with dealing with the hurts and pains of relationships. We are to deal with them before they become bitter roots. Those kinds of hurt feelings and broken relationships cause people to miss the grace of God. We have to be committed to a character that reflects the generous portion of grace Jesus demonstrates. Our commitment to that level of grace is a commitment to His holy character. We choose reconciliation because to choose otherwise is to warp the reflection of His heart in our spirit.

No Need for Damaged Love

Something powerful happens to our relationships when we experience this kind of unbridled grace. Liz received this kind of reconciliation from Joe. His unconditional patience restored the passion of their love. I wish you could see Liz's eyes when she talks about her husband who waited for her. Her eyes fill with tears as she looks at him with a deep and abiding love. He proved there is nothing she could do that would cause him to abandon his love for her. She knows she didn't earn it. That makes their love that much more precious. It is God's gift to her through her husband. It reflects the heart of Christ who died for us while we were still rejecting Him.

I am not suggesting that we should choose to go through painful periods of our relationships so that we can know the amazing passion that results from being so unconditionally loved. Love does not need tragedy to be unconditionally expressed. However, I am suggesting that tragedy doesn't require us to live in damaged love. The love of God is powerful enough to restore our relationship to completeness. Our love for one another doesn't have to be diminished just because it has gone through pain and suffering. It can be resurrected to complete and full love.

Reconciliation is difficult because it calls us to walk away from fairness and all its comforts. Reconciliation in the Kingdom chooses to pattern itself after Jesus. That's why we don't wait for the other party to initiate the journey. We knock. We call out for healing. We patiently wait. And when the other person opens the door we fulfill our promise and enter into the journey of healing so that we can enjoy the gift of relationship.

8
GENEROSITY AT CHURCH
ctto

Manipulation Isn't Generous

I was young in ministry and thinking I had learned enough leadership training to handle most situations. This particular conversation caught me off guard and left me sickened by my response.

I had been to breakfast with a church member I'll call Jake to discuss various needs within the church. Jake was generous to the church with his finances, and whenever I needed something really big, Jake usually stepped up and helped. God had blessed his ability to make money and he had given significantly to the church on many occasions. We had just instituted some major plans and, once again, I asked Jake to step up.

What I didn't realize was just how lonely Jake had become. His financial blessing intimidated the other men at church, and it was difficult for Jake to make solid friendships. I'm sorry I was not more attentive to his needs.

I was getting ready to get out of the car. "Jake I want to thank you again for all the help you've been. I couldn't have pulled this off without your help."

Jake grew solemn. "I wanted to talk to you about that, Pastor. I'm frustrated. Nobody in the church ever talks to me. I feel as if the only reason they even pay attention is because of my money. I can't do it anymore. I'm counting on you to help me. If I don't start making some friendships, I'm going to leave the church."

I understood his frustration and even sympathized with his need to find a fellowship of believers that loved him for who he was. But, his next comment stunned me. "If I go, my money goes with me. If that happens, your project won't happen at all."

Astonished, I heard myself utter the words "I understand you are hurting. I will do my best to help you." I wish I could tell you my response was a response of grace. The truth is I was dumbfounded and really didn't know what to say. I was hoping I had misunderstood the apparent threat that had just been made.

It took me several days to come to grips with what had happened. With each passing day I grew angrier. This parishioner was committing extortion with God's resources. Bit by bit I came to the realization that Jake had never really been generous. All these years he had been purchasing power and position. His money had been a bully club he wielded, and the church was his latest victim.

If/Then Demands

Jake's story, while severe, is a reflection of many of our own stories. We give at church only to the extent that we receive something in return. We may never be so bold as to verbalize the threat. However, our threat is just as real. "If nobody cares enough to notice I cleaned the restrooms, then someone else can clean them!" "Why does it seem as if I'm the only one who cares enough to give for that cause? I'm tired of it. Someone else can take care of it next time."

You fill in the if/then statement that fits your frustration. "If they don't . . . then I won't. . . ." "If this doesn't happen, then I am going to. . . ." When we limit our generosity to the extent to which we are repaid for our generosity, we are not generous at all. We are back-scratchers.

We each want different kinds of repayment. Some of us have to receive applause to be willing to keep giving. For some, the repayment comes in the form of a position. We love to be the ones in charge. We want to be the one who gets his or her way. We want influence.

For some, our repayment comes in the form of attention. "That pastor never visits me. I bet he'll be coming to talk when I stop paying my tithe to his church!"

I realize it all sounds very selfish. If we hadn't all been guilty of one or more of these acts of reciprocity, it would sound almost ridiculous. However, it doesn't take too much time hanging around the church to realize these attitudes aren't uncommon at all.

In fact, they are some of the very attitudes that are keeping the church from experiencing the overflowing power of the Spirit as He pours himself out through the church onto our communities. It doesn't matter how powerful our spiritual gifts were intended to be, when the love that empowers our gifts is diluted by this kind of reciprocity, nobody sees Jesus in our behavior. Others get a taste of our demanding spirits, and it doesn't taste very good at all.

When Jesus instructed us to give, He warns us from seeking a reward from any other source than the Father.

> Be careful not to do your "acts of righteousness" before men, to be seen by them. If you do, you will have no reward from your Father in heaven. So when you give to the needy, do not announce it with trumpets, as the hypocrites do in the synagogues and on the streets, to be honored by men. I tell you the truth, they have received their reward in full. But when you give to the needy, do not let your left hand know what your right hand is doing, so that your giving may be in secret. Then your Father, who sees what is done in secret, will reward you. —Matthew 6:1-4

Jesus is talking about *attitude*. Are we doing what we do so that others will reward us with power, position, praise, and the like? Or are we responding to the grace of God in our lives? When we do what we do because we love God, He rewards us. We have to be honest with ourselves about our tendency to demand repayment for our generous acts.

Finding the Joy in Giving

When we give to get, we rarely give joyfully. We give with a host of expectations. When those expectations aren't met, our disappointment turns to anger. When we live under this cycle, giving is drudgery.

Paul calls us to "cheerfulness" in our generosity.

Each of you must give as you have made up your mind, not reluctantly or under compulsion, for God loves a cheerful giver. —2 Corinthians 9:7 NRSV

God is the motivation for our giving. When He is the only one we are paying attention to, and our giving is an act of worship, generosity is full of joy. We can choose to give sacrificially because we are aware of just how sacrificially Christ gave to us.

Think about what a slap in Christ's face it is for us to accept His sacrifice on the cross and then demand that we receive attention, power, position, or applause because of the small ways we give. We must acknowledge the sinfulness of our tendency to demand special treatment for our sacrifice. It is time to retake the posture of worship—to bow before the cross in gratitude of the one who died for us.

When it comes to church, there are several areas in which we struggle to maintain an attitude of true generosity. While we are going to touch on a few of them, keep in mind that generosity at church is simply choosing to give regardless of whether or not those who receive our gifts deserve or appreciate them. We choose to give of ourselves out of reverence for the sacrificial love of Christ. We should be doing that at home, at church, at school, at work, everywhere. Generosity isn't something isolated to church. However, church provides some unique opportunities to shift from generosity to reciprocity. So, we need to take the time to frankly discuss the temptations.

Generosity of Time

Scotty was a quiet man who did more for the church in a week than most people did in a year. He had come to the Lord late in life, but he served Christ as someone who deeply felt the debt of love he owed. On any given week, Scotty mowed the churchyard, cleaned the church building, and fixed three or four broken parts on different pieces of church property.

He never complained about church problems. In fact, one time Scotty came to me and said, "Pastor Kevin, if you don't tell me the things the church needs, how am I supposed to help?" Scotty never accepted a dime from the church, yet he gave an average of twenty hours a week all the years I pastored him. His heart overflowed with a kind of servant attitude I had rarely seen in others and had never seen in myself.

Scotty's example isn't unique. There are millions of Christians across the globe giving countless hours every week to their churches. But, that doesn't make it generosity. Our giving becomes generosity when we give our time without demanding anyone give us recognition. It becomes generosity when our time is given out of a deep love and gratitude for what God did in us. It becomes generosity when we keep giving our time, even when others refuse to.

We live in a day when time is one of most precious commodities we possess. Families are pressed with little league, school activities, long work hours, and a host of many things that rob us of balance. It's important to find a balance between family, work, church, and rest.

It is important to look to Christ's sacrifice and give of ourselves without demanding public acknowledgment or any sort of reciprocity. The reward will come; however, the reward will come from Christ.

Giving Up Positional Power

When we spend so much time among a small group of people, we tend to get the idea that all of life is made up of that one group. Inside that social microcosm we put a great deal of emphasis on our position—even at church.

We wield our power and position as weapons to get done what we believe is best. We can easily forget that leaders in the Kingdom are called to be servants. We find so much personal validation in our positions that we walk away from Christ's example of washing our feet.

I've pastored and consulted for twenty years. I have seen countless individuals become angry because they weren't elected to the board or appointed to this or that committee. I've seen the disgruntled expressions on church members who show up to find some visitor has had the audacity to sit in their seats. I've watched longstanding church members grow increasingly frustrated with their diminishing influence because of a sudden influx of new members won by a charismatic pastor. They don't even understand their own emotions; they just know their opinion is no longer as valued as it once was. They are upset, and they are going to make sure someone hears their complaints. They've worked too many years in their church to be disregarded like that!

The tendency to limit our generosity, our willingness to give of ourselves to the extent we maintain our power, is nothing new. Jesus was confronted with His own apostles' thirst for power.

Jesus has just announced He is going to Jerusalem. His apostles don't understand He is heading to His death. They think He is finally going to rise to power. At this possibility, the lust for position throws the apostles into a fight. In Matthew we read of their thirst for power and Jesus' call to servanthood.

Then the mother of Zebedee's sons came to Jesus with her sons and, kneeling down, asked a favor of him. "What is it you want?" he asked. She said, "Grant that one of these two sons of mine may sit at your right and the other at your left in your kingdom." "You don't know what you are asking," Jesus said to them. "Can you drink the cup I am going to drink?" "We can," they answered. Jesus said to them, "You will indeed drink from my cup, but to sit at my right or left is not for me to grant. These places belong to those for whom they have been prepared by my Father." When the ten heard about this, they were indignant with the two brothers. —Matthew 20:20-24

It is amazing that even before the first church was established, families were vying for control. This mom comes with her two sons and asks they sit in the seats of power, the left and right. Little did they know those seats were to be taken by two thieves. I doubt very much they would have been so eager for the position had they known the level of sacrifice it would require.

We mimic their boldness more than we would care to admit. We herd up in families and fight anyone who wants to keep us from our right to tell the church what to do. Then just like the other apostles, the church grows indignant that we would dare try to take the position and power they are convinced is theirs. The fight is on.

From Jesus' day to now, we have listened to Jesus' instructions at the end of this passage, and have tended to ignore them. I want to encourage you to stop the fighting for position and listen closely to Jesus' instructions about leadership in the church. It is leadership based in sacrificial generosity, not reciprocity.

> Jesus called them together and said, "You know that the rulers of the Gentiles lord it over them, and their high officials exercise authority over them. Not so with you. Instead, whoever wants to become great among you must be your servant, and whoever wants to be first must be your slave—just as the Son of Man did not come to be served, but to serve, and to give his life as a ransom for many." —Matthew 20:24-28

Leadership in the church isn't supposed to look like the positional posturing we often see in the realm of politics and business. We aren't to *lord over* people, but to *serve* them. Greatness in the kingdom isn't defined by powerful positions, but by powerful service. We are to model Christ who came to serve us, not force us to serve Him.

Our culture has become so indoctrinated into the world's understanding of prestige that we can't see the butler as someone who is honored. It isn't considered honorable to pick up the trash or clean the toilets. It's considered honorable to be recognized as a key leader, a generous donor, a person of influence.

Of course, there is nothing wrong with being a key leader, a generous donor, or a person of influence. It is wrong to approach generosity at church as a power play.

Focus on Lost People

Generosity at church is to model Christ who "came to give his life as a ransom for many" (Matthew 20:28). We choose to keep giving because people need Jesus.

You may remember that in the first chapter I referred to a period where I grew increasingly frustrated with church. I was working hard on many fronts and was feeling pretty sorry for myself. I was convinced I was giving more, serving more, working more than anyone else, and I was tired of it.

I had gotten so frustrated that I even began hating going to church. I knew that from the time I entered the building to the time I left, I was going to be hounded by one person after another for help with one thing or another. I was burning out on church.

After the Holy Spirit confronted me with my lack of generosity, I did some serious soul searching. I had to find my motivation for going to church. I was entering the phase of life when others were going to turn to me for help. Gone were the days when mature Christians were my support. I had now joined their ranks and was expected to constantly give to others.

After several months of prayer and soul searching, I found a motivation that overcame my selfishness. I saw the faces of many young adults who I knew needed to be encouraged to stay faithful to Christ. They were living on just a little money or were going through the pain of learning how to be married.

They were new to the whole adult responsibility thing and were more than a little overwhelmed and hurting. I even remember saying to myself, *Even if you don't get a thing out of going, those kids can't afford for you to stay home.*

I started waking up on Sunday mornings far more motivated to get to church. I knew they needed Christ, and I knew I needed to help them find Him. I knew what they had been through, and I knew they could stay faithful to Christ if they received the encouragement they needed.

My reason to keep giving was the heart of Christ pouring out in me. He loved those people desperately, and once I got over my self-absorbed focus on my own needs, I found joy in meeting theirs. Christ was beginning to transform my back-scratching behavior into Christlike generosity.

It's About Christ, Not Methods

I once thought the reason churches failed was because of faulty methods. I am beginning to believe the methods don't mean nearly as much as the attitudes of the believers practicing them. It really doesn't matter whether you like hymns or choruses, whether you think the pastor ought to be a shepherd or a rancher, whether you like small groups or large groups, whether you like liturgy or worship teams. If your attitude says, *It's my way or the highway,* you've missed the heart of Christ who left everything He knew to walk a new journey designed to reach lost people.

Paul dealt with just such a group that had allowed its allegiance to different leaders to grow into a fight. In the first chapter of 1 Corinthians, Paul addresses some folks who are quarrelling about whose leadership they followed, and he reminds them they are to follow Christ.

> For it has been reported to me by Chloe's people that there are quarrels among you, my brothers and sisters. What I mean is that each of you says, "I belong to Paul," or "I belong to Apollos," or "I belong to Cephas," or "I belong to Christ." Has Christ been divided? —1 Corinthians 1:11-13

Paul goes on to remind them that their methods of ministry really don't matter and shouldn't be cause for fights. He reminds them they aren't to boast in anything but Christ.

We must be careful to not allow differences in methods to become divisive. You can choose to demand your way be followed. You can choose to limit your servanthood to those times when people do ministry the way you want them to. That doesn't reflect the heart of Christ.

Jesus reminded us that people are drawn to him when *He* is lifted up. We can get so committed to our methods, that we lose our generous spirit. We serve as long as our methods are followed, but when someone wants to try something that doesn't fit with our preferred methods we fight back.

I had introduced some new music to a little church I served early in my ministry. I really thought I had done these wonderful people a true service by bringing some life to their otherwise stale worship.

Sally met me at the back of the sanctuary. I smiled, "Hi Sally! What did you think of the new songs this morning?"

I'd never seen a senior citizen truly angry before. The sight was disturbing; she was almost shaking. She put her index finger right in my face and told me what she thought. "You better bring back my hymns, young man. You better bring back my hymns!"

I laugh now, but at the time I was quite shaken. I never stopped to think that the method of worship would mean so much to this dear lady.

Before we find fault with Sally's emotional outburst, we must admit we have all done similar things. We are radically committed to what we are used to. It's comfortable; it feels right, and when somebody messes with it we get upset.

Here's my point. We must be careful to avoid the temptation to use our power to push people around when the methods change. It is during these times of transition that we tend to forget our call is to serve, even when we are uncomfortable with the changing culture within the church. Generosity at church often means supporting the next generation as they do ministry in ways that makes sense to them. That is easy to say when we are the ones making the changes. It is difficult when our kids are "messing with church."

You Won't Miss What Isn't Yours

My mother-in-law loves to tell the story of her father's church and its miracle year. The little country church had suffered under a poor economy. They were a church of farmers, and life wasn't easy. The church never had enough money, and the people were frustrated with their apparent inability to gather enough offerings to keep the church in the black.

One of the members was a grain elevator owner. He was a successful businessman the church people trusted, so they approached him about taking over the treasurer's position. If anyone could turn this thing around, he could.

"I will take the job with one condition. For one year, you can't ask me any questions. I promise you, we will fix the financial difficulties. But, as we do, I don't want anyone bothering me with questions about how I am doing it."

In today's cynical age, we would wonder if this old farmer was asking us to turn a blind eye to unscrupulous behavior, but this was an old country church and they trusted their friend. "Okay, you have a deal."

During that year, the church quickly turned around financially. Before long, the church had not only caught up its bills, but also had a pretty extensive surplus. It was one of the best financial years the church had ever experienced.

At the end of the year, the people were quite curious. They had to know how the grain elevator owner had fixed the church's financial woes. His answer redefined generosity for this little church. "Every time one of you farmers who regularly attend this church brought your grain to my elevator, I went into my office and calculated how much I owed you for the grain you were delivering to me. I wrote that number down, subtracted God's ten percent, and then paid you the remaining ninety percent that was yours. I then took God's ten percent and put it in the offering on Sunday. You never complained about tithing, because you didn't treat it like it was yours to begin with. Within a short time, the church had more than enough to meet the needs."

The church people were a little embarrassed by their obvious unfaithfulness. At the same time, they were astonished at what simply following the scripture's call for generosity in our giving could accomplish in a short time.

When we choose to see our money as our own, tithing feels like a tax. We hate giving away what is rightfully ours, so we lose the cheerfulness that flows from a heart filled with gratitude. We love our money more than we want to worship God. That kills our financial generosity.

Remember: generosity is the decision to give as Jesus gave to us. He didn't limit His sacrifice based on what we deserved. He generously poured himself out on us because He loved us and wanted us to know the Father.

I would suggest to you that this is the secret for becoming a cheerful giver through our tithes and offerings. We aren't cheerful because we have sacrificed something; we aren't cheerful because we gave to people who really deserved our generosity.

We are cheerful for a couple reasons. First, we have walked away from a worship of material things and have finally begun to trust God more than His blessing. Second, we fully believe in the evangelistic work of the church and know that can't happen without our investment. We have a way to make a difference in the lives of people we love by providing the resources necessary to run those ministries that are changing lives.

Ministry as Generosity

I sat in front of the class as we finished up the six-week course on spiritual gifts and ministry in the church.

"The good news is that you are now beginning to understand your spiritual gifts. That means you will be able to focus on your strengths and stay away from those areas of ministry God never intended for you. However, I want you to be aware of something. From now on, you will always give more than you receive. You are moving from a worship that is based on what others give you into a worship that is based on what you give to others. Don't worry though. This is when your worship becomes rich and deep."

I was trying to help this young adult group understand something about ministry and the church. When we are young, others minister to us more than we minister to others. We are growing in our faith and learning a great deal about how to follow Christ. However, something happens in us as we mature and develop in Christ. Church quits being about what we are getting and shifts to being about what we are giving. Our spiritual gifts start driving our worship experience. We can't worship without ministry.

When my wife and I left pastoral ministry, we started attending a large church. Week after week we attended Sunday School, sat in worship, and left. Our children were involved in big, thriving youth programs. The church had plenty of resources. On the surface, it seemed like a good thing. However, we were not connecting to the church. We couldn't understand why we were so frustrated. We were mature believers; we weren't supposed to feel this way.

After several months, my father called. He pastored a church nearby and was trying to get a worship team up and running. He knew we had some experience with this and asked if we would come over to his church for a few months to help. The few months turned into six years of service. We served that church until God called us back to pastoral ministry.

My wife and I have both led worship teams, taught Sunday School, served on committees, done renovation on different parts of the building, and much more. We still get frustrated with church, but that's just because there are people involved. We give of ourselves because we care.

What was the difference? Why did we connect with one church and not the other? In the larger church, we made the mistake of waiting to receive something. When you sit back and expect the church to do something in you that makes you connect, you are ignoring Paul's teachings on spiritual gifts. We connect with people when we give of ourselves to them. That is how God wired us. That is how the Holy Spirit operates within us. When we serve others, we worship. When we try to worship without service, we spiritually dry up and die.

When God's Generosity Shines Through Us

Generosity at church flows from spiritual gifts. Paul begins to explain the issue in 1 Corinthians 12:7 when he writes, "Now to each one the manifestation of the Spirit is given for the common good." He is referencing spiritual gifts. While the work of defining and identifying spiritual gifts has been undertaken by many other volumes and will not be undertaken in this one, it is important to note that spiritual gifts are directly linked to the choice to reflect the generous character of God.

When I utilize my spiritual gifts at church, people don't see me; they see God. When I teach, encourage, show faith, administer a program, or serve dinner to the senior citizens, God is using my action to manifest himself to others. His light shines through my actions, so others sense God rather than me.

God made us that way. He put these spiritual gifts in us for the good of those we serve. Whereas our talents are simply natural abilities that may or may not lift up others' spiritual lives, spiritual gifts always help other people draw closer to God. God put spiritual gifts in me because He expects me to give of myself to others so that they can see more of Him.

When I am at church, and I choose to serve within my spiritual gifts, I am choosing to allow God to give of himself to others through my actions. My spiritual gifts are actually a form of God's generosity being poured out on others around me.

I pastored full-time for fourteen years. It took me quite a while to come to grips with the idea that God didn't intend for me to be everything my congregation needed. He had given spiritual gifts to every believer in the church, and He never intended for me to take their places.

When I realized that God hadn't gifted me in the areas of caregiving and nurture, I experienced an emotional freedom that allowed me to help my church members experience all God had for them. I gathered around all those who had the spiritual gifts of caregiving and put them in charge of the day-to-day shepherding of the flock. They kept me informed of when I was really needed. For the most part, these people met the caregiving needs of the congregation.

If I had been so stubborn as to believe that I should have been the one who gave these people what they needed, regardless of whether or not I really had what they needed, my self-ishness would have kept our congregation from getting the doses of God's Spirit they needed.

Choosing to be generous at church doesn't mean you have to do everything. Being generous at church means you have to ask God how He has gifted you and then do all you can to allow God to minister to others as you operate within His design for your ministry.

We all feel worn out from time to time. It is then that we need to find Sabbath and spiritual renewal. We must refuel our spirit with God's Spirit. It is only the Holy Spirit flowing through us that allows us to be channels for God's mercy. There are times we need to stop and just let Him fill the tank.

However, if I choose to live a life of only receiving from the Holy Spirit, and never allow Him to flow through me to touch others, then I am not experiencing God's purpose for my life. I am, in fact, withholding from others the very things they need to be able to experience God's presence.

When I spoke earlier of the young adults in my church as the motivation God used to reignite my fervor, this is what I was talking about. My spiritual gifts were given to me so that those young adults could connect with God. I find my purpose, my reason for giving, by recognizing that God intends for my church experience to be about helping others.

When I focus on my spiritual gifts as a way for God to help others, I am learning what true generosity looks like. I am partnering with God in His desire to draw these people to himself. He has chosen to do that through my gifts, and I should treat that as an amazing privilege.

This is when ministry becomes worship. I look at God and praise Him for what He has done in my life. I see that He wants to show himself to others through my generosity. So I choose to honor God's call on my life. I worship Him as I pour myself out on those around me. I worship through ministry. I choose to give, even when I don't feel like it and others don't deserve it. I choose to give because I know God wants to reveal himself to others and has chosen to accomplish that through my spiritual gifts.

Generosity Is More than Money

Too often we look at generosity at church and interpret it only as a money issue. We know we should give with smiles on our faces, but the scripture teaches that generosity is the character of Christ flowing through our behavior. Don't get me wrong. You can't claim to be generous and then be stingy with God's resources. But generosity goes way beyond the simple issue of being faithful with our tithes and offerings.

Church is to be a place where people can come just as they are in order to begin a relationship with God. Too often it becomes a soap opera of families fighting for one form of control or another. We must look at Christ's example and choose the kind of generous grace that finds fulfillment in washing our neighbor's feet.

The power of the church is Christ. When we lift Him up by choosing to sacrifice ourselves out of the same love that drove Him to the cross, God's generous character is made evident to those who are seeking Him.

9
GENEROSITY IN THE WORLD

Beyond Christmas Bells

I love Christmas. Some years I'm ready for the decorations the day after Thanksgiving. Some years, I'd prefer to skip Halloween and just start baking cookies early. There is something about the season that brings out the best in people.

The holidays are a time when many people are moved to donate funds to help others. Something happens to us as we begin to focus on Christ in the manger. It brings us back to the gift of God and reminds us that we are to reflect His generosity.

I'm not among the bah-humbugers who cynically condemn those who give at the end of the year. I think it is good that we are at least reminded that life is not all about meeting our own needs. However, I do believe we must be careful not to confuse periodic acts of kindness with the generous character of God that causes us to continually give of ourselves regardless of what we get back.

It's Just Who We Are

If our acts of generosity reflect the Pharisees who sought public recognition for their kindness, we have missed the heart of the Father. When our character reflects the generosity of

God on a daily basis, we are quite surprised that anyone would consider our actions extraordinary.

It is a serious issue with eternal consequences. In Matthew 25 Jesus describes two groups of people. One group is surprised that they have offended God; the other is surprised that their actions were somehow worthy of praise.

When the Son of Man comes in his glory, and all the angels with him, he will sit on his throne in heavenly glory. All the nations will be gathered before him, and he will separate the people one from another as a shepherd separates the sheep from the goats. He will put the sheep on his right and the goats on his left. Then the King will say to those on his right, "Come, you who are blessed by my Father; take your inheritance, the kingdom prepared for you since the creation of the world. For I was hungry and you gave me something to eat, I was thirsty and you gave me something to drink, I was a stranger and you invited me in, I needed clothes and you clothed me, I was sick and you looked after me, I was in prison and you came to visit me." Then the righteous will answer him, "Lord, when did we see you hungry and feed you, or thirsty and give you something to drink? When did we see you a stranger and invite you in, or needing clothes and clothe you? When did we see you sick or in prison and go to visit you?" The King will reply, "I tell you the truth, whatever you did for one of the least of these brothers of mine, you did for me." Then he will say to those on his left, "Depart from me, you who are cursed, into the eternal fire prepared for the devil and his angels. For I was hungry and you gave me nothing to eat, I was thirsty and you gave me nothing to drink, I was a stranger and you did not invite me in, I needed clothes and you did not clothe me, I was sick and in prison and you did not look after me." They also will answer, "Lord, when did we see you hungry or thirsty or a stranger or needing clothes or sick or in prison, and did not help you?" He will reply, "I tell you the truth, whatever you did not do for one of the least of these, you did not do for me." Then they will go away to eternal punishment, but the righteous to eternal life." —Matthew 25:31-46

True generosity flows out of our character. It is just who we are. And so, when we see someone in need, we try to meet the need. When we see someone hurting, we try to help. It isn't extraordinary. It's the way things should be. We don't come before God and claim to deserve anything in return for our goodness. The irony is that God rewards such an attitude of generosity.

On the other hand, when we walk through this world focused on our rights, completely unaware of the needs of those around us, we are in trouble. God confronts us with the reality that He doesn't even recognize himself in our character.

Religious Activity Isn't Generosity

Sometimes we neglect our need to show this kind of generosity to the world around us and we justify our ungodly character by our religious activity.

Not everyone who says to me, "Lord, Lord," will enter the kingdom of heaven, but only the one who does the will of my Father in heaven. On that day many will say to me, "Lord, Lord, did we not prophesy in your name, and cast out demons in your name, and do many deeds of power in your name?" Then I will declare to them, "I never knew you; go away from me, you evildoers." —Matthew 7:21-23 NRSV

It is not enough for us to do "the church thing" and then never meet the needs of our neighbors. Jesus declares that He never knew us. His character was never reflected in ours. He wants to look at us and see His generous love reflected in our behavior. It doesn't matter if we preach the word, cast out demons, or perform miracles. If we are stingy with our resources and refuse to help those in need, our religious activity cannot serve as a replacement for the holiness of God's love.

Jesus talked about this defining difference between religious people and those who reflect the character of Christ. In the end it comes down to our behavior.

"What do you think? There was a man who had two sons. He went to the first and said, "Son, go and work today in the vineyard." "I will not," he answered, but later he changed his mind and went. Then the father went to the other son and said the same thing. He answered, "I will, sir," but he did not go. "Which of the two did what his father wanted?" "The first," they answered. Jesus said to them, "I tell you the truth, the tax collectors and the prostitutes are entering the kingdom of God ahead of you. —Matthew 21:28-31

Jesus is confronting the Pharisees. They've got the religious act down. But they are still disobedient to the heart of God. They are so committed to their position and power that they refuse to find the transformation Christ wants to deliver. Their example shows it isn't enough to know what is right, we have to act on it.

Here is what Jesus is really teaching us. It doesn't matter that we call ourselves followers of Christ. What we say about our stand before God doesn't really make it true. What we do on a consistent basis is the evidence of who we really are.

Dr. Ken Hendricks was one of my professors at Olivet Nazarene University in the 1980s. He was a military man and was prone to saying things bluntly. One day in class he clarified this issue for me in one statement. I'll never forget his words. "Gentlemen, don't tell me what you believe. I'll know what you believe by how you live." That is what Jesus is getting at. We can't claim to possess the heart of God and then choose to ignore the needs of the world around us.

A few weeks ago, I was discussing this issue with a pastor. He asked me, "Kevin, is generosity an activity or an intent?"

"Neither," I replied. "It goes beyond intent, and it isn't just an activity. Generosity is character. Intent and activity are necessary. But they are the result of true generosity, not the cause."

Many people want to reduce generosity to an idea. If that is all it is, then we can look at our next-door neighbor's need and feel good about the fact we are concerned. If generosity is less than character, we can get away with the emotional response of empathy.

Generosity goes way beyond our intentions. Moreover, it isn't simply an activity. It is the heart of one who has been so loved that he or she is now characterized by the unconditional love of God.

When our hearts have been transformed, we cannot look at our neighbor's need and *do* nothing. We cannot look at our neighbors need and *feel* nothing. We will hurt for the hurting and deliver the cup of cold water in Jesus' name. We do this because that's who we are—followers of Christ, who lavishly poured out His love so that we could experience a changed life.

Principles of Generosity in the World

There are two primary places that we interact with the world around us—work and community. These two venues comprise the "world" for most of us. While they each have their unique challenges, there are a few principles of generosity that can be applied to both.

Reflecting the Character of Christ

Paul is admonishing us to live a holy life with these words.

And whatever you do, in word or deed, do everything in the name of the Lord Jesus, giving thanks to God the Father through him. —Colossians. 3:17 NRSV

Whatever we do, in our speech and in our work, we are to give of ourselves as a representative of Jesus Christ. Our attitude is to be one of gratitude. We give our best because that is who we are.

I have had the privilege of serving in both the church world and the secular world. I have seen people who approach their jobs as a central part of their ministry, and those who see their jobs as chores to be completed as quickly and painlessly as possible. I've watched church leaders treat their neighbors as if they were trash. I've watched the most inconspicuous believers become beacons of hope for neighbors who are deeply hurting.

Generosity in the world means choosing to embrace the heart of God who gives when it isn't deserved. We keep investing in the lives around us regardless of their gratitude. We do this because our service is to the Lord, not the recipient of our generosity.

More than "Expected"

I teach some business courses for Indiana Wesleyan University. One of the classes focuses a great deal of time on servant leadership as Christian business people. The class was filled with young adults already in their careers.

I began the night by saying, "If you will listen to what I am about to tell you, three to five years from now you will look around and people will be turning to you for leadership and direction at work." Some eyes grew wide, and others grew thin with skepticism.

"If every day you go to work, you will do just a little more than others are willing to do, if you will learn a little more than others are willing to study, and if you give of yourself to help somebody else become better than they were yesterday, you will rise up in leadership."

Anna was a young lady who seemed to be eating it up. She listened intently and asked questions as the lecture went on. When class was over she came up and asked some questions to clarify her understanding.

My time with those students came to an end, and I was glad to have had the opportunity to dump a little help into their lives. Several months passed, and I was teaching another class. I learned that one of the ladies in my new class was Anna's cousin. I asked her to tell her cousin hello for me.

The next week she returned to class with a message from Anna. "She said to tell you thank you for what you taught her. She took your lesson to heart and started doing the things you had challenged her to do. She has had three promotions since the end of that class!"

Anna had learned the principle of generosity in her workplace, and as a result God was raising her up in leadership. I'm not saying that if you are generous your life is going to be a series of promotions. What I am saying is that when we choose a generous spirit, it stands out against a back-scratcher world. When others are asking, "How much do I have to give?" you are looking for ways to invest more than is expected. God will use that to transform the hearts and minds of those you serve. In turn, they will look to you for leadership.

Looking for Ways to Make Our World Better

When we are living generously we are alert to ways to make the world better. The Holy Spirit creates in us a heart for people. Generosity is so much a part of us that our generous acts don't seem especially extraordinary to us. In fact, we are often surprised that God is able to do something through our feeble efforts.

Brad Odell is a Christian father in Louisville, Kentucky. Like many men, he had saved his pennies for a rainy day and had gathered several hundred dollars. He was a new Christian, and his local Christian radio station was part of his daily spiritual diet.

The station he listened to was holding its three-day fundraising event and Brad decided he should help. He took his young son with him to the station to make their twenty-dollar-a-month pledge. His son, Devon, made a two-dollar-a-month pledge. Brad walked away gratified that he had done something generous and that his son was learning a good lesson early in life.

As Brad listened throughout the week, it was evident the economy was impacting the station's ability to raise the funds they needed, and Brad was feeling the tug of the Holy Spirit to do more to help. But what could he do on his truck driver's wage?

By the third day, Brad was convinced God was asking him to do something sacrificial, and he was pretty sure what that meant. It wasn't going to be easy; a man's rainy day fund is a precious thing.

Brad took Devon and headed to the bank. He withdrew the six hundred dollars it had taken him a long time to save. *God, are you sure about this? This is a lot of money. What will my wife think about me just giving it away?* Brad bought two three hundred dollar grocery cards and headed to the radio station.

He spoke with the radio station personnel and told them he believed God wanted him to give the cards to use in their fundraising effort. "Are you sure?" they asked. "I'm pretty sure God told me to do it." Brad handed over the cards

A few minutes later the on-air staff announced they were going to try to raise five thousand dollars in fifteen minutes. Everyone who donated during the next fifteen minutes would be included in a drawing for the groceries. Brad was stunned. He had been listening to the station steadily, and he knew that kind of money hadn't been raised all week. His nerves kicked in as he sat in the lobby and listened. "I sure hope I did the right thing."

After six or seven minutes, the phones were barely ringing. Brad's knees where shaking. The staff must have been getting nervous too. The host got on the air. "Now folks, I'm sitting here looking at these cards, frustrated because I can't be a part of this. You know, three hundred dollars will fill two grocery carts."

The phones started ringing off the hook. Employees were running down the hallway to answer calls because the audio booth phones were overflowing with donations. At the end of the fifteen minutes God had used Brad's generous spirit to perform a miracle in the life of the radio ministry. They raised over nine thousand dollars from Brad's six hundred dollar gift!

Sometimes we make the mistake of believing that because the needs of the world are so massive we can't make a difference. We believe our limited resources won't make a dent in the world's needs. For most of us, that's true. But God can use our loaves and fish to bring a miracle into our circles of influence when we listen and trust His call. We can't control the breadth of need around us, but we can control our willingness to do what God asks of us.

It's important to identify those things God has called us to impact and then do what we can to meet the needs we see. We will never meet all the needs, but to live out the generous spirit of Christ is to offer the resources God has given us to make a difference in the way God has ordained.

Rather than offering excuses of what we can't accomplish, we must trust God to do more with our resources than we believed possible. When we look for God's guidance and choose to see life as an opportunity to worship him, our lives become the offering He uses to affect change in our world.

Eric lost his father when he was six years old. His mother remarried while Eric was still in elementary school. His stepfather suffered medical problems and was unable to work. By the time Erik was sixteen, he was working to support his family.

Life hadn't treated Erik fairly, and it wasn't easy for him. No one would have blamed him if he felt bitter. Yet God was using these difficulties to form a generous heart in Erik.

When Erik shared his story there was no hint of bitterness in his spirit. In fact, he now leads groups of fellow university students in compassionate ministry efforts. They gather food for the food bank. They serve at the local homeless shelter. They are even organizing events for mentally challenged children. I asked, "Why do you do all of these things?"

His reply was a reflection of the generous spirit of Christ. "I figure I have suffered a lot of things. So, I really feel God wants me to help others who are also suffering. This is how I worship."

That is what generosity in our world looks like. It looks like people choosing to give rather than demanding repayment. It looks like young men and women who give of themselves when others would curl up in a fetal position and accuse the world of evil intent. This kind of generosity reflects joy on the faces of those who embrace it.

✳ ✳ ✳

For most people, their generosity in the world will never appear grand to others looking on. Most will never have a building named after them; most will never be mentioned in the halls of philanthropy. Most of us will live our lives in obscurity. However, we can all live a life of great impact when we choose to give as Jesus gave.

Whether at work or in our communities, we can make the choice to meet the needs we see within the resources God delivers to us. We can give more than is expected and forgive more than is deserved. We can choose to make our lives about lifting others up, refusing to consider ourselves important. We can look at Christ's sacrifice and choose to model His generous spirit. When we live this life of generous love, and walk away from our culture's back-scratching values, we will become a beacon of hope God will use to impact this world for Christ.

CONCLUSION

Jesus taught generosity that flows against the basic rules of fairness embraced by a world that thrives on reciprocity—giving only in the measure received. Jesus says we should walk an extra mile, turn the other check, and give our tunic as well. But deep from within our sense of justice, we cry "Unfair!" We have been trained by a culture of back scratchers. "You scratch my back, and I'll scratch yours." I'll give, if it seems fair to do so.

From the time we were children, we quickly learned what was fair. If I give you my toy, you have to give me yours. We know that it is okay to share, as long as we get something in return. We know that it is okay to give, as long as the person receiving reciprocates. And in this "you scratch my back, and I'll scratch yours" culture, we have lost the central focus of Jesus' call to transformational generosity.

As much as we want to show the same kind of generosity displayed for us on the cross, we are limited by our commitment to "equity"—I will only give an amount equal to what I receive in return. We do not express true generosity, but reciprocity. And so, our servanthood at home, church, and the world is limited by our desire to get something back for our sacrifice.

However, Jesus calls us to accept one source of reciprocity: we love him because he first loved us. Every other act of generosity is to be an expression of gratitude for his unbridled grace.

More than that, our generosity is a reflection of his character. The call to be holy as He is holy demands we embrace generosity in our relationships.

Living generously will change how I deal with my spouse and children. I am to serve them out of reverence for Christ. I will treat my spouse as a gift from God. I will lavish grace on my children as I discipline them into a knowledge of God's holiness.

Christ-like generosity changes how I deal with conflict and reconciliation. Like Christ, I stand at the door of my enemy and knock. I remain open to the possibility of God's grace healing the sin that separates me from my brother. I give up my right to walk away, while holding firm to the need to fix the issues that have caused the separation.

Reflecting Christ's character will change how I express generosity at church. Rather than limit my ministry based on how I am applauded or how much others sacrifice, I choose to serve out of the same sacrificial generosity from which Jesus serves me. Whether giving money, time, leadership, or love, I will do so because Christ loved me first. I refuse to demand repayment for my generosity because I am a debtor to Christ's love for me.

True generosity changes how I meet needs in the world around me. In a world that gives in order to receive public recognition, I refuse to trade the recognition of the Father for accolades from men. Embracing Christ's teaching will change how I express generosity at work. Rather than give only what I am paid to complete, I will give more than is expected. I will invest in those around me. I will become a source of change by leading through service.

And so, I must make a choice to accept my only source of reciprocity—Jesus' sacrifice for me. I will wash my hands of a system in which I must be paid for my generosity. I will embrace a generous life that is an expression of gratitude for the transformation Jesus brought to me. And out of reverence for what Christ has done for me, I will generously serve those He loves.

"Dear Jesus, help me walk away from a world driven by reciprocity and embrace the generous grace of God, who sent His Son to die in my place."

BIBLIOGRAPHY

Anastasi, Tom. (1995). *The Fight Free Marriage*. Nashville, TN. Thomas Nelson Publishers.

Chapman, Gary. (1992). *The Five Languages of Love*. Chicago, IL. Moody Press.

Rath, Tom. (2009) *How Full Is Your Bucket*. New York, NY. Gallup Press.

Harley, William F. (2001). *His Needs, Her Needs*. Grand Rapids, MI. Flemming H. Revell.

Black, M., Martini, C. M., Metzger, B. M., & Wikgren, A. (1997, c1982). *The Greek New Testament*. Federal Republic of Germany: United Bible Societies.

Green, J. B., McKnight, S., & Marshall, I. H. (1992). *Dictionary of Jesus and the Gospels*. Downers Grove, Ill.: InterVarsity Press.

Theological Dictionary of the New Testament. 1964-c1976 (G. Kittel, G. W. Bromiley & G. Friedrich, Ed.) (electronic ed.). Grand Rapids, MI: Eerdmans.

Kittel, G., Friedrich, G., & Bromiley, G. W. (1995, c1985). *Theological dictionary of the New Testament*. Grand Rapids, Mich.: W.B. Eerdmans.

Liddell, H. (1996). *A Lexicon: Abridged from Liddell and Scott's Greek-English lexicon*. Oak Harbor, WA: Logos Research Systems, Inc.

Louw, J. P., & Nida, E. A. (1996, c1989). *Greek-English Lexicon of the New Testament:* Based on semantic domains (electronic ed. of the 2nd edition.). New York: United Bible societies.

Nestle, E., & McReynolds, P. R. (1997, c1982). *Nestle Aland 26th Edition Greek New Testament with McReynolds English Interlinear*. Oak Harbor: Logos Research Systems, Inc.

Newberry, T., & Berry, G. R. (2004). *The Interlinear Literal Translation of the Greek New Testament*. Bellingham, WA: Logos Research Systems, Inc.

Schwandt, J., & Collins, C. J. (2006; 2006). *The ESV English-Greek Reverse Interlinear New Testament*. Logos Research Systems, Inc.

Schwandt, J. (2004; 2004). *The NRSV English-Greek Reverse Interlinear New Testament*. Logos Research Systems, Inc.

Strong, J. (1996). *The Exhaustive Concordance of the Bible:* Showing every word of the text of the common English version of the canonical books, and every occurrence of each word in regular order. (electronic ed.). Ontario: Woodside Bible Fellowship.

Swanson, J. (1997). *Dictionary of Biblical Languages with Semantic Domains: Greek* (New Testament) (electronic ed.). Oak Harbor: Logos Research Systems, Inc.

Throckmorton, B. H., Jr. (1997, c1992). *Gospel Parallels—NRSV:* A comparison of the Synoptic Gospels. Nashville: Thomas Nelson.

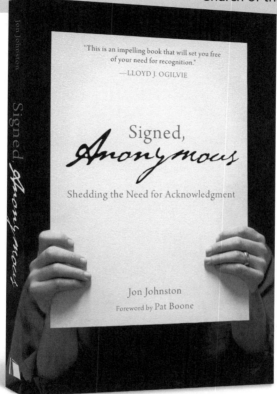